Speaking with Confidence

About the Author

Nick Gold is the Managing Director of Speakers Corner, a leading global speaker bureau, which over twenty years has built a network of over 7,500 speakers internationally. He is Director of Speaking Office, a keynote speaker management company. He is the president of the International Association of Speaker Bureaus (IASB) and was formerly the Chairman of the European Association of Speaker Bureaus. Nick has spoken at major industry events including Confex and The Business Show and has been published extensively across UK media outlets including the *Telegraph*, *City AM* and *GQ*.

Nick Gold

Speaking with Confidence

BUSINESS

PENGUIN BUSINESS

UK | USA | Canada | Ireland | Australia
India | New Zealand | South Africa

Penguin Business is part of the Penguin Random
House group of companies whose addresses can
be found at global.penguinrandomhouse.com.

Penguin
Random House
UK

First published 2020
001

Copyright © Nick Gold, 2020

The moral right of the author has been asserted

Set in 11.75/14.75 pt Minion Pro
Typeset by Jouve (UK), Milton Keynes
Printed and bound in Great Britain by
Clays Ltd, Elcograf S.p.A.

A CIP catalogue record for this book is available
from the British Library

ISBN: 978–0–241–46817–3

Follow us on LinkedIn: https://www.linkedin.com/
company/penguin-connect/
www.greenpenguin.co.uk

To my dad, Lawrence Gold, who will forever be in my thoughts and gave me the belief and guidance to have a voice and speak with confidence

Contents

Introduction

You *can* speak with confidence. If you follow the pointers and tips in these coming pages, I have no doubt you'll become an accomplished public speaker. That may sound like a bold assertion but I'm absolutely convinced it's true. Everybody can learn to speak well.

Despite this, many people are scared of getting up to talk in front of an audience. There's even a technical term for this: glossophobia. It's so common that it's believed to affect up to 75 per cent of the population, with an estimated 10 per cent of those at the more extreme end of the spectrum. If you are one of the many who make up this number, it may strike you that your glossophobia is insurmountable. It isn't. With the right preparation and support, you can overcome your barriers and stumbling blocks. In the following chapters I will help you look at speaking in a fresh way that will dissipate much of the anxiety and put you in control. I say 'much', rather than 'all', because some nerves are a good thing. Harnessed in the right way, they bring the necessary energy to your performance. They help you to focus and connect.

One of the fundamentals of successful public speaking is to understand that, no matter how good at it you become, it's always the audience that is the star. They're the focus. Not you. Later on in this book, I'll explain how this works and how to use it to your advantage – because by truly understanding this, you can boost your self-confidence and performance. I'll also be exploring why public speaking is most definitely not one-way traffic. The best speeches mirror a conversation, and actively provoke interaction and reaction. The goal should always be to:

- engage with your audience, and
- deliver a lasting impact.

Time spent in front of an audience actually delivering a speech is only part of the picture. So, I'll be breaking down the speechmaking process into 'before', 'during' and 'after', all of which are vital stages in ensuring your message hits home. This includes aspects such as creating an environment in which you feel comfortable. A large degree of success comes down to proper preparation.

One of the notable things about wonderful speakers is that there are no stereotypes. They come from a wide variety of backgrounds, and their personalities vary enormously. In fact, their individualism makes them good at what they do. That's because being true to yourself is at the core of successful public speaking. Which is all the more reason to believe me when I say that anyone can do it.

You can do it.

I have been fortunate to pursue and enjoy a career that has immersed me in the world of speaking. I am the Managing Director of Speakers Corner, which has grown to become one of the biggest speaker bureaux in the world. We work on more than 1,000 events a year, and have over 7,000 speakers on our books. Alongside Speakers Corner, I co-founded the speaker management business Speaking Office, with my brother Tim

Gold and Michael Levey. My work is all about supporting people to overcome any fears or barriers they might have, and to make the most of their talent.

So, as well as my thoughts and theories, this book is packed with insights from some of the fantastic speakers it's my pleasure to work with on a regular basis. What they have to say is honest, illuminating and very practical. This is a golden opportunity to learn from some masterful exponents of speaking who have been generous in sharing their 'trade secrets'.

Together, let's banish glossophobia.

It's time for you to become a glossophile, blessed with the skills and confidence to hold an audience in the palm of your hand.

1. Show and Tell

Most of us have an innate fear of public speaking. We worry we may not be up to it; that we'll freeze, stumble over our words, bore the audience or make mortifying mistakes. We will learn, throughout this book, that this fear may never completely subside. But you will learn how to control it, work with it, and use it to your advantage when speaking in front of groups. The title of this book is *Speaking with Confidence*, but that is not to suggest that speaking is something only the super-confident can do. Quite the contrary: speaking is something everyone can do, whether you feel confident or not to start with. I want you to believe in yourself. Because you can do it – and do it well.

Step 1: Belief

We all start life speaking confidently. And that undoubtedly includes you. But, over time, as we get older – and supposedly wiser – we acquire a tendency to feel more apprehensive about public speaking. Our mature, rational brain suppresses the imaginative capabilities of childhood and allows fear and reserve to creep in.

We were all at primary school once. Back then, we used to be excited by Show and Tell, when we could bring in our favourite thing to talk about. We'd stick our hand in the air and wave it about frantically, hoping to catch the teacher's eye while willing ourselves to be picked. If we were lucky enough to be chosen, we'd rush to the front of the class and proceed to regale and entertain our peers with stories of why the particular item held a special place in our life and why it was so important. Each of us, in our delight to show and tell, was a natural orator, entertaining and engaging an audience eager to hear more.

Looking back at these carefree situations, we should ask ourselves, why were we able to do this? What gave us the confidence to stand up and speak without weeks of preparation, stress and overthinking? Even more pertinently, what kept our audience interested and engaged in our most prized possession? For any would-be speaker, in any situation, the answer to this is the first step in giving yourself the best chance of success: belief.

The person delivering the Show and Tell is talking about something they believe in, something they care about with genuine passion. They use their own words, rather than words read from a prompt or written by someone else. This allows them to bring to life a story that is *their* story, suffused with their own experience and personality.

CASE STUDY

Will Butler-Adams: Natural enthusiasm

Will Butler-Adams, boss of Brompton Bicycle and Brompton Bike Hire, and a well-respected public speaker, is a fan of this sort of approach. He warns not to 'overly curate' your words, so that your natural self will shine through. 'Because if you over-curate, it's like you're reading from a textbook – and it's stilted, and it's not you. So, if what you're saying isn't you, then you're probably not going to be relaxed doing it.'

In this way, enthusiasm is not an act or forced. It's a natural enthusiasm that's intoxicating and outward-facing. Which means that the audience, in the grip of your passion, comes along for the ride. They want to be part of the adventure.

I appreciate that all of the above can be easily dismissed or ignored. After all, I'm talking about Show and Tell at primary school. A time when our lives lay ahead of us and we were unburdened by the stark realities of the adult world. And before we worried about being judged by our audience. Before we had to consider how the way we act in front of other people might have a massive impact on our career prospects, credibility and reputation.

It's no surprise, therefore, that adults see greater risk in public speaking than our younger selves would have done. However, while I think we should all aspire to keep hold of the enthusiasm for life and adventure we had as children, that's not the main point of conjuring up memories of Show and Tell. Show and Tell is to remember that we all have the belief in ourselves; sometimes we just need to rediscover it.

Step 2: Ownership

The aspect I'd now like you to zero in on is the ownership of the content. The way your younger self would have passionately owned what you said to your classmates about something that really meant something to you – whether that was a favourite

Star Wars toy, an idolized pop singer's autograph, or the chewed-up frisbee you threw time and again for your adored family pooch.

What does this mean for the speaker who wants to stand and deliver with confidence? It means you must believe in – and, more importantly, *own* – the content that you will be sharing with your audience. And by content we don't necessarily mean the raw data. When it comes down to it, if you're delivering a business presentation, there's a strong possibility you won't be the only person involved in coming up with the content. Normally, at least some of the presentation will be created through teamwork. But even so, you can still own it. To do that, you have to wrap your own experiences and personality around the information so that it really means something to you. The more you as a speaker can tell your own stories, while weaving in the messages you need to deliver, the more engaged the audience will be.

Of course you must be careful not to shoehorn in messages or anecdotes in a manner that feels forced and jarring. But always remember, your audience wants stories. They are human beings, first and foremost, not just buyers, regulators or peers at an industry event, and they will respond positively to emotion they can relate to and invest in. Give them that and they'll be receptive to the messages you're aiming to deliver.

Moreover, and critically for a speaker, once you personalize your speech with your own stories, it becomes an event which you can embody completely. That will give you a massive confidence boost. As you move on to the comfortable ground of telling stories about yourself, of sharing glimpses of your personality, speech-giving nerves and fear will evaporate.

Gemma Milne: Combining insight and passion

Gemma Milne, a young Scottish science and technology writer and podcaster who has become an inspiring keynote speaker on subjects as diverse as biotech, health, advanced computing, space, energy and innovation in academia, was thrown in at the deep end for her first speech when, only nine days into a new job, her boss asked her to give a presentation on innovation to 500 people in Dubai. As it was a 45-minute slot, she felt it would be boring to spend all that time focusing on the role of her company's innovation team. So she decided to combine one of her passions with some insight into what motivates people.

'I did a whole section on what is it that makes people tick? That's what's really important when it comes to advertising,' recalls Gemma. 'So I did a whole section on how I love maths, showing little number tricks. I was trying to show people how amazing maths is – my goal in life is to make everyone love maths – and I was basically saying, "This is what makes me tick, and understanding what makes other people tick is x, y, z."

'After I did that one, I got really good feedback. I knew that I wanted to be able to mix not necessarily my story, but awe and wonder and asking questions – and that sort of naive optimism that is very me – into any topic that I ever did. I had no interest in corporate presentations. Yes, I wanted to share my love of maths and share my sense of wonder, but I also knew that was what made me interesting.'

That self-awareness and passion has undoubtedly shaped Gemma's approach to her public-speaking career. 'I think sometimes with a talk people want, "What are the nine steps to . . . ?" Whereas with other kinds of talks it's, "How do I rethink this particular industry or concept or idea?" ' she says. 'Anyone can learn how to do either, but I think your expertise and your preferences tend to make you fall into one. I certainly fall into the, "How do I plant a seed and make people think for themselves?" as opposed to, "Here's my experience, copy it." '

What stories can you tell about yourself that feel genuine and share a glimpse of your personality? What are the parts of your life – hobbies, heroes or heroines – that you can talk about unselfconsciously? What would be your subject on *Just a Minute*? What makes you unique? Because these are all the details that your listeners will find interesting and will make your speech memorable.

Speaking tips

- Be the passionate owner of your content.
- Take your audience on a journey.
- Channel your inner 'Show and Tell'.

2. What's Your Brand?

The world is full of brands. They're everywhere. From the cars we drive to the clothes we wear; from the tech we use to the packaged food and drink we consume; from the financial products we buy to the airlines with which we fly. All of them are carefully managed brands, with qualities we recognize and relate to. And we all have our favourites. Brands we trust for their performance and dependability. Or connect with because they are in tune with our values, aspirations and the way we live our lives.

None of this happens by accident. Product and corporate brands are rigorously nurtured and promoted. Teams of people work hard on positioning and communication, making sure that what a brand stands for is expressed in the right way and delivered to the appropriate audience. For many companies, brands are their most valuable assets.

When the word 'brand' is applied to people, it's automatic to think of those celebrities who are instantly identifiable by their first names or nicknames. Beyoncé, Adele, Posh & Becks, Rihanna, Ant and Dec, CR7 . . . These stars have a brand that reflects the persona they are trying to present to the world. On hearing their names, we recognize not only who they are but also what they represent.

Personal brands aren't just the domain of celebrities. We

each have our brand or persona. But we don't usually think of ourselves as a brand, because most of the time we are simply getting on with things, while feeling comfortable with who we are. We have our network of friends and family who know us, so we don't feel the need to position ourselves in order for them to recognize our 'brand attributes'.

Even in the more formal setting of work, we generally go into meetings on the understanding that we are representing the brand or values of the organization we work for. The people we meet may have already drawn conclusions or made presumptions about what we are doing in the meeting and how we are positioned. But when we are speaking in public, whatever the format or environment, we have the opportunity to go further. So, it's imperative that we position our personal brand in the right way, in order to lay the foundations for the message we are going to deliver in our speech.

The importance of body language

Effective public speaking hinges on far more than just the words you're going to say. Over the years, the relationship between verbal and non-verbal communication has been discussed and debated, and it has been consistently agreed that body language matters a great deal. Our posture, gestures and other movements are instinctively read by others, and they make an impression on our audience when we speak in public.

Whether they like to admit it or not, people form judgements – on whether they like us or want to take on board what we have to say – based on our body language. And our tone of voice, too. The actual text of our speech and the literal meaning of our words are only one part of the picture.

While that's no more than common sense, it can be easily overlooked. Many speakers fail to take into consideration that how you speak and move form a major part of your personal brand, and as such can exert immense influence on your audience.

As we saw in the previous chapter, successful public speaking is all about authenticity. Your persona onstage or in front of an audience cannot be a manufactured identity. While you might be able to contrive a fit with the words and content you're delivering, ultimately your speech will fall down if it is not in line with your personal brand. Your audience will smell a rat. For an example of disconcertingly out-of-character body language, it's hard to outdo former Prime Minister Theresa May's now notorious arrival onstage at the 2018 Tory Party Conference to the strains of Abba's *Dancing Queen*. Her awkward dancing was in such stark contrast to her usual public persona that her audience, and the national press, responded by calling out her inauthenticity (to put it kindly).

CASE STUDY

Rory Sutherland: Staying true to yourself

Someone who's very good at staying true to his personal brand is Rory Sutherland, the self-styled 'Cinderella of Advertising'. Rory has had a long and illustrious career in advertising, marketing and branding and is an in-demand public speaker on topics such as technology and the future of advertising. Onstage he tends to speak fast and aims to be entertaining, which is how he is in daily life.

'Generally, I try to be fairly similar from offstage to onstage,' says Rory. 'I never get enhanced salesmanship, because I think it's counter-productive. Your talk should give product demonstration, but it shouldn't be a sales pitch. I believe that very sincerely. And that makes me, therefore, more comfortable speaking. Because I'm not comfortable doing a hard sell. It's not my temperament to do that kind of thing. I'd much rather prove something, and demonstrate it.'

In general, a disconnect between the words delivered and a speaker's personal brand equates to a high risk of failure. There will be the odd exception. Gifted actors, for example, will be able to deliver content convincingly in a variety of styles – it might be said that the various characters a talented thespian is able to portray are akin to different brands. And when it comes to intonation and physicality, they're the pros. Those of us who aren't Oscar winners or theatrical heavyweights can't possibly match that, so we should stick to being ourselves.

Identifying your personal style

Understanding your brand and thus your style is a great starting point for the creation and delivery of a speech. But what does that entail? It might sound daunting, yet it isn't. To begin, all you have to do is ask yourself what makes you feel comfortable? Think about how you like to say and do things. What you're aiming for here is to get a strong sense of your natural persona. The more you plan and prepare with this in mind, the more at ease you'll feel when you get up in front of an audience. Being mindful of 'brand you' leads to harmonious speechmaking that's in tune with your personality. When you practise, you'll pick up on what's out of keeping – whether that be in terms of content or delivery style.

Conversational habits

A good tip for boosting your self-awareness is to look back on recent conversations you've had with friends, for instance when you've met them in cafes, restaurants or on a virtual hangout.

- Are you the one who tends to lead the conversation?
- Are you challenging or provocative in your opinions?
- Do you have a way with a funny anecdote?

These are just some examples of the questions you might ask in order to gain an insight into your conversational style. Try to appraise yourself as accurately as you can.

The 'five words' challenge

Of course, people act in different ways in different circumstances. So, to get a rounded picture, approach a selection of friends and family members whose judgement you trust and ask them to describe you in five words. There should be some overlap – or at least some close similarities – in the words chosen by those close to you. Like it or not, these are attributes of your brand – which cannot help but be defined, to some degree, by the perceptions of others.

If a character trait comes up that you really don't like, you may choose to work on improvement in this area (although this really is a topic for another kind of book). Where I can help you is in harnessing the positive and neutral adjectives that people have used to define you. Own these in exactly the same way that you should be owning the messages of your speech. Allow them to inform how you construct the text and delivery of your speech, which is just another way of saying 'play to your strengths'.

Taking it onstage

When it's time to speak, you will be bringing your own brand attributes onstage with you in your head. Adhering to your natural persona will ensure the style and content of your words ring true, setting your audience – as well as yourself – at ease. Let's take a look now at how some of the most experienced speakers do this.

The power of exaggeration

Having accepted and embraced their persona, the best speakers take an exaggerated version of themselves onstage. They pick the bits of their persona that will most benefit them in their delivery of the speech, and then exaggerate them in front of an audience.

Again, it's worthwhile stressing that these aren't newly manufactured attributes. Rather, they are elements of themselves that they dial up in order to deliver the best possible performance. I have enjoyed watching many accomplished speakers, and what's noteworthy is that they are able to remain very comfortable because the way they deliver their speech always stays 'on brand'.

CASE STUDY

Jez Rose: Keeping it real

'Sincerity is critical: be real,' says Jez Rose, magician, broadcaster, motivational speaker – and owner of the world's first carbon-neutral bee farm. 'If you're not, you'll find it very difficult to juggle effectively multiple personalities, and the result will be a clunky client journey.'

Jez also urges people not to force themselves into a widely available mould. 'Just because everyone and their dog talks about customer service, it doesn't mean you should.' As to his personal brand, Jez describes his onstage persona as a 'heightened and more energetic version' of himself. Like me, he's adamant that it's critical for your brand to align well with content and messaging.

'It not only looks more professional, and therefore helps build trust in both you and your content, but it demonstrates to your audience that you've put the time and effort in,' says Jez. 'You're asking people to sit and listen to you for [possibly] an hour or more; why should they bother if you couldn't be bothered to put the effort in yourself? It's the small things that often make the biggest difference.'

The importance of preparation

While your chances of success are much higher if the delivery of your speech corresponds with your brand persona, getting your personal brand in order should start far earlier in the process than speech day. A good understanding of your brand when composing your speech will provide clarity and direction as to the style of the speech and how it should be structured.

Always construct your speech with your personal brand – and how you will convey your brand attributes – firmly in mind. As you write, visualize how you will deliver each part of the speech in a way that's natural to you. This will assist both with the flow of what you write and with its delivery when the time to speak arrives.

Delivering the key messages

When you come to weaving in the key messages you want to convey, think of them in the context of your brand and beliefs. Check that how you're expressing your messages complements your brand, rather than conflicting with it.

Here it's worth observing that you won't feel the same level of attachment to all the messages in a speech. Some will be fundamental, even sacrosanct. Others less so. Take some time to think through how those lesser messages fit with your brand. How best can you express these without them feeling forced? The more comfortable you are with them, the better your speech will go, because you'll minimize awkward 'lull' points. These are the moments in the delivery of your speech when you pause, and when you want your audience to feel at ease. That's far easier to achieve if your body language is in line with your messages – something which will come much more naturally if you have taken time to work out how those lesser messages fit with your brand.

If you don't think these things through, in advance of delivering your speech, there's the danger that some of the points you're trying to make will be inadvertently undermined by your own non-verbal communication.

Keeping it believable

No one disputes that the success of any public speech depends on more than just the words delivered. At the speech construction phase, as well as during the actual delivery, the speaker needs to understand who they are and what their brand is. You want to avoid putting yourself in a position where you'll feel uncomfortable or succumb to the temptation to force a persona that really isn't you. That's a big pitfall. Your audience will see through a forced persona, and from there it's not a big leap for them to start wondering what else in your presentation might be false. In their minds, they may begin questioning whether all the information you're sharing with them is genuine and truthful.

Clearly, you want to avoid this sort of outcome. So, use your brand to safeguard your credibility. If you do the groundwork I've outlined above, there's every reason to be confident that your speech will hit the mark.

Speaking tips

- Stay true to what makes you feel comfortable.

3. What's Your Message?

You've been asked to make a speech, run an important meeting, present your research to a group, or pitch for investment. That's great. A wonderful opportunity. But where to start?

Identify the core messages

By planning your speech ahead of time, you are giving yourself the best possible chance of success. In so far as your core messages are concerned, time spent on this part of the process is not only valuable in the short term, for the speech or presentation at hand, but also lays the solid groundwork for future speaking occasions.

In your enthusiasm, you may already have jotted down some ideas. Or perhaps you are staring in frustration at a blank page, hoping for inspiration to strike. Either way, what you need to do first is get some clarity about your core messages: what you want to say. By this I don't mean immediately summoning up a whole speech, point by point, line by line. No, what I'm talking about here are the broad brush strokes.

Generally, there's an intimate relationship between core messages and why you're qualified to share them. Say that professionally you're a quality assurance guru, widely respected and with plenty of experience in your field. That, no doubt, gives you the credentials to wax lyrical on quality control, standards, audits, benchmarks and so forth. There's plenty of detail you could doubtless cover in great depth, where necessary. However, if you were to condense all of that down into the top-line core message, it might run something like this: I really care about quality control, in order to make things safer, better and more efficient.

This underlying core message should be both your starting point and a consistent thread that runs through your speech. And when I say starting point, that applies not only to embarking on the writing of your speech but also often to the content of your opening lines. Here are some approaches to help you get going.

Use openings that capture your audience's attention

Demonstrate your credentials

A useful starting point is to tell the audience what you will be talking about and why you have the credibility to talk about it. As a speaker, you've been invited onstage or are in the position to give your presentation because you have the authority to be there. Embrace that! Appearing in front of an audience, however big or small, is flattering. There's nothing wrong in receiving a boost to the ego. An element of ego gives you the inner strength to stand up and speak. Otherwise, doubts will persist and nag away at you as you build up to your speech. To prevent that happening, focus on the reason why you're the one doing it.

Cherish your authority and be proud of your expertise. Sharing these with the audience will have the same settling effect for them. Consider the following examples.

- If you're making a toast at a friend's wedding, you might start by saying, 'I've known the groom for over thirty years and I'm going to be telling you all some of my favourite stories today.'
- If you are going to present your research to your wider team, you could say, 'I'm head of the marketing team and I've been leading this project for six months.'

Establish your authority as a speaker and let them know that they are in a safe pair of hands. It might sound simple, but it's a good place to start.

Ask an intriguing question

Another opening, and perhaps a more exciting one, is to highlight a problem or question. For example, 'How can your business survive in the age of rapid disruption?' Your aim is to evoke a visceral reaction that captures the audience's attention and gives your speech immediate momentum.

That question about survival can then be tied in to your core message – the assurance that, as a business development or corporate transformation expert, you can help your audience find some answers to the existential threats confronting their organizations.

Harness your know-how and values

Logically, if you are a sports performance maestro, fine art historian or supply chain brainbox, your knowledge and take on your specialist area should consistently inform your core messages, even if the content and angle of each speech you give is different.

What you must bear in mind is that it's not just what you do. It's also why and how you go about it. This is what you want to encapsulate in your core message. In this way, you're not just a fine art historian. You may be a fine art historian with a particular interest in Renaissance sculpture and its parallels with three-dimensional art in twenty-first-century Britain. Clarity of this kind gives you something solid to build on – much as some sculptors use the basic structure of an armature on which to complete a finished artwork.

In one respect, therefore, your core messages may be grounded in your technical knowledge. Yet they should also be an expression of your personal beliefs and values. What makes you, *you*. Why you do the job you do. How you go about doing it and why that matters. What you really care about.

Your values should be at the root of your core messages. In essence, these values are the drivers that relate to your personal brand (as discussed in the previous chapter).

Nailing down your core messages is a big step on the road to creating the content of your speech. It will help the words flow. Moreover, being able to articulate your core messages will also have an impact on your delivery style and format. The key beliefs and values you are looking to put across in your speech will inevitably shape it. But as I say, this does require you to understand them first. Otherwise, you cannot possibly hope to distil them into practical core messages.

Here are some useful questions to help you think about this.

- How do you want your audience to feel?
- Why should they listen to you?
- Do you want to ask questions, or answer them?
- What should your audience take away from your talk?
- If you could only make three points, what would they be?

Once you understand your core messages, the blank page won't stay blank for long. People who've spent a lot of time mulling over their core message may have successfully boiled it down to just a handful of words that encompass everything about them. My favourite example of this is the author and journalist Malcolm Gladwell, whose first book was titled *The Tipping Point* – a phrase and concept that hadn't been heard before in that context, but was immediately recognizable as that moment in time when some act moves from being distinct to being familiar and embedded. Other examples include Jim Collins writing about *Good to Great*, or Simon Sinek's *Start With Why*. All examples of a message distilled down to a handful of words which the reader or listener grasps at some level and instinctively wants to understand more fully. Three cheers for their conciseness! For most of us, though, it's likely to be a few statements that encapsulate who we are, what we stand for and how we act.

At this point it's worth stressing that these statements don't have to be turned into a slick message. It's not about using them verbatim in your speech. Consider them as the structure around which everything can be built. This will aid you in writing and delivering the speech. Most importantly, post-speech, it will help you evaluate whether or not you were successful in meeting your aims – in terms of both the content you sought to put across, and whether you pitched it at the right level emotionally to connect with the people in the room.

Apply the nuts and bolts

Once you have a firm handle on your core messages, you can start thinking about the nuts and bolts of the speech itself. Ask yourself two questions.

- What exactly are you trying to say?
- What conclusions will you draw?

You need to make sure your answers align with both your brief for the speech and the technical know-how and values you have taken the trouble to distil. Contextualizing the content of your speech so that it's in keeping with your core messages will give it identity, character and a life which sits comfortably with your ideals, aspirations and personality. I can't emphasize enough how important it is to stay true to you.

This is where you take a strategic view of what you need to prepare, and begin marshalling the ideas, tools and information that will feed into your speech. Be sure to set yourself clear objectives based on your brief but also on the values you want to convey. You should be clear on what you're hoping to achieve from the speech, from your own point of view but also for your audience. What would success look like from their perspective? Try to articulate and visualize the reaction you want from them.

CASE STUDY

Colin Maclachlan: Clear, relevant and memorable

Former Special Forces soldier Colin Maclachlan, star of Channel 4's reality TV drama SAS: Who Dares Wins and Channel 5's Secrets of the SAS, is an accomplished speaker on topics including resilience, teamwork, leadership, risk, motivation, conflict resolution, change management, negotiation and performance. Colin has three rules concerning core messages. They must be clear, relevant and memorable.

'Whenever one is developing a core message, think about how your experience and that of others applies, and how to make a neat fit between your story and the people you are speaking to,' advises Colin. 'This may seem a leap when it comes to comparing Special Forces missions with the day-to-day running of a business, but the process and techniques are very similar. Most talks are between twenty and forty minutes, as that is probably the length of time we can actively hold someone's attention. So, think about the main points you want to get over in that time. Think bang for your buck! Concentrate on how it runs and make sure it doesn't go off piste. Stick to the subject!

'Vary how you tell the core message so it is a mix of your experience and how other more well-known [histories] have proven what you're saying. This also helps in terms of interesting facts that the audience may not have known. For example, most of the top one hundred successful entrepreneurs have failed around ten times for every one great idea they have had.'

Taking raw content and contextualizing it in line with your personality is a big step towards harnessing the enthusiasm and authenticity of the Show and Tell positivity discussed in the first chapter. It's that essential *ownership* of the content that we've already talked about. Your aim should be to write a speech owned by you, the speech maker, not only from a content perspective – you're delivering the message you set out to deliver – but also from an emotional perspective. That means delivering the message in a way that is comfortable for you, feels part of you, and allows you to be invested in it emotionally as well as intellectually.

CASE STUDY

Miles Hilton-Barber: From the heart

World record-breaking adventurer Miles Hilton-Barber, sightless since his early twenties, is an inspiring public speaker with a well-earned reputation for speaking from the heart.

'Just tell them what you think,' he urges. 'What's in your heart. And that could be very different to what other people have been saying and doing. The big thing is your message, not your profile. What is the point in being like everyone else? In your message and your speech, you don't have to be fancy. You want it to come from your heart. And if it does, you'll reach people.'

Miles can't be faulted for speaking from the heart. It's absolutely the right way to go about it.

Let's circle back to staring at that blank page. With your message in mind you're now primed to create something powerful. Writer's block will be less of an issue because you already have clarity on some of the things you want to express. Revisit the questions earlier in this chapter, if you're still struggling to get your core messages straight. However, assuming you're clear on these, use them as a litmus test for the words you write. Do they ring true? Are they representative of who you are? Is this genuinely content you're proud to *own*? If it isn't, rework it until you no longer have any misgivings.

Debra Searle: Repetition, simplification, reduction

Renowned businesswoman, author and TV presenter Debra Searle, who toughed it out to row solo across the Atlantic Ocean, has given over a thousand speeches. Now, when writing a presentation, she tries not to think of her audience as a body of people, preferring to imagine them as one person – an 'avatar', as she puts it – because she finds this really helps her with message construction.

'You have an individual in mind,' she says. 'You're writing almost for that one person. And I find that quite a helpful way of bringing the story to life, because you're thinking about, "If I stood with that person in a pub, having this story, how would I speak to them? And what would I want to leave them with?"'

Once you've decided on your key messages, Debra has three tips for driving them home: repetition, simplification and reduction.

Simplification means distilling messages down to a phrase or word (that you keep repeating, of course). Reduction means being sure not to burden the audience with copious amounts of unnecessary detail. Far better to deliver key nuggets of information that they will retain in their minds, take away with them and, ideally, apply to their lives and jobs.

If you express them well, your core messages can and will help and inspire others. You want them to hit home, to have a lasting impact. For some lucky people oratory comes easily. They seem to have been gifted with natural skills. But even the most intuitive and fluent orators can put themselves in a position of vulnerability if they neglect to take a step back and give some proper thought to what they really want to say. For those who aren't natural orators, honing your messages gives you the best possible chance of making an impact.

Turn pre-speech nerves to your advantage

It's fine to feel somewhat nervous ahead of delivering your speech. Every speaker should expect to experience an adrenaline spike, or other manifestations of nerves. You should embrace these feelings, because they are perfectly normal. A bit of adrenaline will help you focus, and you can channel it into your performance in a positive way. If you do find yourself in the grip of pre-speech worries, remind yourself of that all-important question: *why?*

Run through your underlying message. Building a speech using your core messages as the foundation will reflect who you are. You know yourself inside out, so you can and should be comfortable in your own skin. And if you're comfortable, you can feel confident. Tell yourself that!

All will be well once you get up onstage and start speaking in your own words, and in your own personal style. It really will be. Stay true to your message, and the moment you start speaking your nerves will be forgotten.

That's my message. Be sure to know and believe in yours.

Speaking tips

- Core messages should be the starting point for your speech.
- Remember to lean on both your technical knowledge and your values.

4. Telling Stories

There's a common strand shared by all great public speakers. This aspect of their speaking ties them together and elevates the speeches they make into the realms of the memorable. They tell stories.

The wonderful thing about telling stories is we can all do it. It's something we all respond to. Actually, it's something we do every day of our lives. We all tell stories.

Yet if stories sit at the heart of great speeches, why is it so often the case that someone planning a speech, especially in a business setting, feels the best way forward is to bombard an audience with statistics, facts and data? Yes, it is absolutely understood that information establishes credibility. It ensures a speaker can stand in front of an audience and be considered an expert in the field they are talking about. However, there's an enormous drawback to any speech where the focus is on delivering as much information as possible, and that is: the person delivering the speech will struggle to connect with their audience at an emotional level. And as we've already seen, that's vitally important.

The power of storytelling

Telling stories is a win-win game. All parties involved have a shared objective that is met through the common strand of storytelling: the speaker tells their stories, the audience can enjoy those stories and, as a consequence, the speech becomes a great success.

A growing body of academic work has emerged in recent years that highlights how effective storytelling can be. Scientists who have explored the brain networks involved in the telling and hearing of stories assert that: 'Skilful storytelling helps listeners understand the essence of complex concepts and ideas in meaningful and often personal ways.'*

People listen and respond to stories, which makes them ideal carriers of messages. So, while a story may not be the most direct way to deliver information, taking the time to weave the facts you want to convey into a story people want to hear will deliver far superior results. After all, would you want to suffer through somebody inconsiderately firing a series of bald statistics at you? Of course not. While a speech of this kind may be shorter in duration, it will probably feel a whole lot longer. And not in a pleasant way. As for the intended key takeaways, how much are you really likely to retain without a good story to help imprint them in your memory?

CASE STUDY

Nick Jankel: Story-crafting

Nick Jankel, an expert in leadership and personal development and author of the international bestseller *Switch On: Unleash Your*

---

* Scientists Wendy A. Suzuki, Mónica I. Feliú-Mójer, Uri Hasson, Rachel Yehuda and Jean Mary Zarate, 'The Science and Power of Storytelling', *Journal of Neuroscience*, 2018, 38 (44), 9468-70.

Creativity and Thrive with the New Science & Spirit of Breakthrough, has worked as an adviser to organizations as diverse as Novartis, LEGO, Nike, 10 Downing Street, the State Department, Oxfam, Unilever and the BBC, and is a very popular keynote speaker on futurism and innovation. He advocates 'story-crafting' every speech to make sure your story hits certain levels and points – what they call 'beats' in Hollywood.

In his opinion, stories should have a strong beginning and end while being coherent and consistent throughout. Deciding on a good metaphor and getting the right organizing principle running through the story are also important. For example, are you trying to tell a story in which the small person beats the big person, like David versus Goliath, or Apple taking on Microsoft in 1984? Or is your story one of redemption? When you set about crafting your story, pay attention to the archetypes, characters and messaging to make sure they are all fit for purpose and not over-complicated or contradictory.

'Essentially for me, a story is painting a pathway of possibility,' says Nick. 'That's what I use often. Because if you're telling a story and there's not going to be a change, there's no need to tell the story. So, all storytellers are essentially trying to create change. If you're an elder in a tribe, you're trying to get the young people to be more ethical – wiser, better, less fighting, whatever. If you're a company and you're trying to get people to do something a bit different, better or new, you may be creating a new future, a new company, new innovation. All stories are essentially change. So, your story has to, at minimum, answer why your current story isn't working or is at the end of its life, and why the new story is better.'

Building an emotional connection

Storytelling transforms a factually based lecture into something of substance that's relatable. Not only will a speech that makes good use of storytelling resonate in the instant, capturing the audience's attention as you're delivering it, but the best points will lodge themselves in the brains of your listeners. The association of information with stories creates a permanent link between the story and the facts, assisting recall.

For the speaker, this is the gateway to success on many levels. Storytelling centres on engagement in the moment. You'll create energy in the room as the audience becomes emotionally invested in the stories you tell. Without necessarily realizing it, they have joined you on a narrative journey. And once they are on board for the ride, you have guaranteed success in the room.

As previously touched on in Chapter 2, 'What's Your Brand?', it's also a critical tool for any speaker who is delivering information to which they are not 100 per cent committed. Most of us have been there: those times in our lives when we've found ourselves in a meeting room, talking on behalf of a team or a company about information that either doesn't excite us or, at worst, that we may not fully believe. Or perhaps you've taken part in a social event where you've had to deliver a speech extolling the virtues of someone or something which you're not wholeheartedly on board with? I can imagine you don't regard the idea of facing such a scenario again as very enticing. But it doesn't have to be a bleak prospect. Quite the opposite.

The thing is, by encompassing the message within a story you can achieve two distinct wins for yourself.

- First, you can turn a message that might strike you as dull – and therefore runs the risk of being delivered without enthusiasm – into something that can be delivered with verve and zest.
- Second, the actual message can be as opaque or definite as you prefer, in order to strike the right balance between fulfilling the objectives of the speech and maintaining the necessary energy and engagement with the audience for the speech to be well received.

Another heartening point to bear in mind is that by going down the storytelling route as a speaker you're putting yourself into an environment that should feel natural. Human beings are a species of storytellers, stretching right back to the narrative imagery of prehistoric cave paintings. Through millennia, we have created legends and parables, told engrossing tales, made up jokes that have characters and mini plots. Today, more than ever, we all tell stories. Whether it be with our friends, our family or our colleagues, we all use the power of stories to engage, relate, inform, amuse and connect. That's why it's essential to incorporate storytelling into your public speaking.

CASE STUDY

Caspar Berry: The purpose of storytelling

Caspar Berry is a unique keynote and motivational speaker who draws on the three years he spent in Las Vegas, making his living as a professional poker player, and his subsequent career as a successful businessman to take a refreshing look at topics such as risk taking, decision making and innovation. His approach to storytelling in his public speaking is to construct a series of events that contain lessons the audience will take away from his speech. Speakers who come up with stories that do not contain the messages or lessons you want an audience to remember have misunderstood the purpose of storytelling in this context, he believes.

'When you are a speaker, it is all about the point of the story,' says Caspar. 'I mentor quite a lot of speakers now and they often have a fundamental misunderstanding of this. The first thing is, you can have a repertoire. You can have on your shelf twenty what we call stories. And within those stories, each one could be made to illustrate three or four points. It's the way that you tell that story to illustrate the point that is absolutely crucial. It's not the story that matters. It's not what's happening that matters. It's the place within that speech that illustrates what you're trying to say. The reason for the story being in there in the first place, that's the thing that matters. The actual events are completely irrelevant.'

Honing your storytelling skills

As you develop as a speaker, the way you go about storytelling is likely to evolve. Once you have a number of successful speeches under your belt – and perhaps you are now speaking on an increasingly regular basis – you may move away from the security of a tightly scripted presentation to a looser structure, which provides some scope to ad lib. This progression, from practising the recitation of a speech, memorizing it word for word, to a more free-wheeling approach, is a fascinating one. Arguably, it calls for an even greater appreciation and utilization of storytelling skills.

Unscripted digressions are fine, but you must never lose the storytelling thread. You should always remember the journey: its purpose and destination. What are the beginning points, the end points and the key points you need to make along the way? As long as you are able to express these well, your narrative doesn't have to be set in stone. Instead, it can take on a life of its own and turn into something more fluid – in particular, when you harness the energy of your audience.

The trick to making this work is knowing your overarching storyline inside out. When you do, how you get from A to B, then B to C, and onwards in your story need be neither prescribed nor rigid. This means that you could give the 'same' speech numerous times but every time the experience would be different – both for you, as the speaker, and for the audience. Once you're comfortable with your story, you'll be able to tell and retell it, with subtle variations from your original script or previous deliveries of a speech on the same topic.

One of the best ways to improve your storytelling is to go and see stand-up comedians. Pay attention to how they weave their set together and the stories they tell. Even better, if possible, go and see the same comedians again, in the same venue, on the following night. This will help you to understand how the same set – with the same stories and jokes – is delivered in a completely different way, with different responses. The sets are not the same as on the night before, but the story journey is. That's what any successful speaker should aspire to deliver. In this context, a routine should never be routine. And in any case, great storytelling can elevate the mundane.

Speaking tips

- Facts will hit home when woven into an interesting narrative.
- Don't veer off track – make sure your stories convey your key points.

5. Understanding the Audience

One of the great things about speaking is that, if everything goes to plan, you can bask in a brief period of public praise and recognition. Speaking publicly is one of the most effective ways to improve your visibility in a team or department, and can fast-track you for promotion. A natural consequence of this attention and approval is that any speaker may feel they are the focus or star of the speech. But I am here to shatter that illusion.

The truth is, it's all about your audience. They are the most important people in the room. They are the ones who determine the success, or otherwise, of your speech.

Needless to say, you have a very strong influence on how your speech will be received. But the audience is the final arbiter. The audience is the 'star', not the speaker.

That's actually a very good thing. Because once you have accepted the fact, it helps take the pressure off your shoulders. You can tell yourself not to be concerned about stage fright, as you're not the star attraction. Try it! It really does help put what you're going to do into perspective.

Make sure you're fully briefed

Shifting the focus on to the audience is a handy way of settling your nerves, but there's far more to it than that. For a start, it underlines the importance of understanding the group of people you'll be speaking to. You certainly don't want to form an impression of your audience based on guesswork. The right way to go about getting a sense of who they are and what they want is to go through a briefing process. The word 'briefing' may conjure up images of a formal meeting or telephone call to discuss the event. While that might be the case for certain types of events or conferences, in reality briefing can take a number of forms. In essence, what we're talking about here is gathering critical information that will help you structure the style of your speech and inform its content.

To prepare, a speaker should ascertain what information they already have to hand and what they need to find out. For example, if you're speaking at an internal meeting or a family event, you will likely already know a fair amount about your audience. It may then simply be a case of bearing in mind what you know already, or finding out a few extra details about a few select attendees. On the other hand, if you've been invited to speak at an external business event you will need to dig deeper.

Over the years, I have heard different speakers pose different questions or frame briefing calls in different ways, but fundamentally they are all looking for answers to the following questions.

- What are the aims and objectives of the event organizer and key stakeholder (who may or may not be the same person) for the whole event, as well as specifically for the speech you'll be giving?

- What are their measures of success for these aims and objectives?
- What is the profile of the audience, and how are they currently feeling?
- What does the event organizer and key stakeholder (but remember, they may not be the same person) want the audience to feel, to say and to do as a reaction to your speech?
- What is due to happen preceding the speech?

By getting detailed answers to these questions you'll gain insight into the context behind your speech, together with a broad overview of what is expected from you. In this way you'll avoid misjudging what your audience wants.

CASE STUDY

Jonathan MacDonald: The U-curve

Entrepreneur and keynote speaker Jonathan MacDonald, an expert in changing business models, says he assiduously does his homework ahead of any briefing call, and always googles the company and recent news about it: 'Any new announcements or changes. If they're a public company, I'll check their stock price. I'll have looked at any major executive movements, so if a Chief Exec has left or a new Chief Exec has come in. I then look on LinkedIn, see if I know anyone that's in the company or used to work for the company.

'Occasionally, I will look on my social media feeds and see if anyone has mentioned the company in a good or a bad way. I will search Twitter to see what the buzz is. If there's a hashtag – because there's a new product, or whatever – I'll then look at the hashtag. I'll search for the hashtag and see whether there are any comments – highly negative or highly positive. What I'm looking for in all of this is what I call the U-curve. If you imagine a U-curve, the top left of the U-curve is extraordinary hostility and the top right of the U-curve is extraordinary positivity and I'm not really interested in the vanilla part at the base of the U. I want to know the really, really bad and the really, really good.'

And the reason for all of this? Because, in advance of the briefing call, it allows Jonathan to work out why the company is running the event. 'Let's say a new Chief Exec has joined in the last twelve months or eighteen months max, there is almost always some form of event that is a team gathering, motivational. Then let's take the opposite version: let's say a particular fast-food restaurant chain has been annihilated online by negative comments on social media. The conference that they have tends to be a people and culture conference which is under the guise of: "We value our team so highly." But it actually is: "We've been smashed online by the public turning against us and the last thing we want is for our staff to turn against us so we're going to run a people and culture event to remind people why it's so brilliant to work here." That trend on the two tips of the U is extremely useful to know in advance of the briefing call. And then, obviously, you get on the call and – surprise, surprise! – the client tells you that they are going to be running a motivational event for senior executives, and you already know why. And it's useful, because then you are pre-briefed before the brief.'

One very important thing to find out about your audience is their level of seniority. For example, it's futile urging people to make sweeping organizational changes if they're not in a position to do so. This is something Jonathan takes very seriously at the briefing stage.

'It's massively critical to consider whether the people in the room can actually do anything about it,' says Jonathan. 'Whether what you're saying is executable by the audience. That's my major audience type: importance. Because if you're speaking to people who are, let's say, the junior team, they're not budget holders, they do not make any critical decisions. Saying to middle management that the company needs to pivot and invest half of its profits into new avenues of innovation is pointless.

'Actually, it's dangerous. It frustrates the audience, because their hands are tied. Equally, when you're speaking to a senior executive team with budget-holding responsibility and you're talking to them about the corporate ladder and how important it is to work your way through the ranks to get to a position of influence, you're speaking to a group of people who have already done that. You're telling them what the last ten years of their job is. It's useless!'

Know your audience's expectations

It's worth pointing out that there might be a number of different stakeholders or people with a vested interest in the successful delivery of your speech. Members of the C-suite will have a different perspective to that of, say, external shareholders in the business. How far you go with respect to understanding the expectations of these different individuals or groups is probably dependent on the importance of the event. But ultimately, the more you as a speaker understand both what is expected from you and the type of environment in which you'll be delivering your speech, the better prepared you'll be – and the greater the likelihood of your speech cutting the mustard.

In truth, it's not only the various event stakeholders who'll have (hopefully, only slightly) differing expectations. To go a step further: whatever the setting, every member of an audience will have a different expectation and objective for the speaker. That doesn't mean you should set about canvassing the opinions of every individual person who'll be in your audience. Even if this were possible, and often it isn't, it would be an all-consuming task with limited value. Nevertheless, there are baseline assumptions you can and should make.

Top of the list is that they want to be entertained. Yes, they may also be looking to be informed, motivated, inspired, and so forth, but their desire for entertainment is guaranteed. No one wants to be bored and disengaged. A hard and fast rule for public speaking is that you have to deliver an enjoyable performance. This brings me full circle, back to the previous chapter on storytelling, the value of which can't be overstated. You need to please your audience through your delivery style and the illuminating and entertaining stories you share with them.

CASE STUDY

Benjamin Zander: Up close and personal

World-famous conductor Benjamin Zander, founder of the Boston Philharmonic Orchestra, who combines classical music with a successful career speaking on leadership, loves to make his audience belly laugh, but cautions it must never be at the expense of anybody else, otherwise you'll lose half the audience. Famously, Benjamin left the stage while giving a TED Talk to get up close to his audience, and his recollection of that incident provides great insight into how important it is to understand and engage with your audience.

'I'm down on the floor and I have a central aisle so that I can go down into the audience and speak to them as if I was speaking to them if I met them in a pub,' recalls Ben. 'Because talking from a stage, God forbid from behind a podium, God forbid reading text, you've lost them from the start. Whereas if you really want to share your enthusiasm about something, you get as close to them as possible and look in their eyes. People often say to me, "I thought you were talking just to me." And so many people say that, that there must be some truth in it. The reason is, I'm constantly looking around, I don't have any notes, no piece of paper, no microphone. I'm walking around, talking as if I'm talking to that person. As if that person really mattered to me, as if I desperately cared.'

I accept that Ben's approach will be too extreme for most. That said, it underlines how speakers can make a lasting impression on an audience with their passion and enthusiasm.

Finalize the style and substance of your speech

Now let's get down to the specific requirements of your speech.

Good preparation is key

The briefing phase is absolutely critical in elucidating what's significant about the context – for example, if you're going to be speaking at a conference, you'll need to find out how your speech will fit in with the overarching theme and with the presentations of other speakers so that you can avoid any unwanted overlap. Does the organizer have any up-to-date delegate information, broader target audience research or sector-specific stats they can share with you? By taking the opportunity to ask these sorts of questions (if they haven't already been volunteered), your briefing with the organizer – and in certain circumstances, possibly a couple of other key people involved in an event – will ensure you come away with a good understanding of the environment in which you'll be speaking as well as what is expected of you in terms of style and substance.

Arrive early at the venue

We'll be exploring more about the actual day of the speech in Chapter 7, 'On the Day'. But allow me to steal a tiny bit of that chapter's thunder by urging you to arrive at your speaking event early, if you possibly can. I've already made the point that briefing doesn't have to be a formal conversation. In fact, briefing could be said to be a continual process leading up to the speech during which the speaker gathers any information which will help them with preparation and delivery. That might pan out as one big formal briefing and a series of mini briefings, with the speaker taking the initiative on the latter.

Arriving early at an event is a great opportunity to immerse yourself in some potentially very useful last-minute mini briefings. You can get a feel for the venue and pick up some vibes as to the tone and mood. If you have the chance to chat to some attendees, you can apply some of what they say or how they behave to your speech. Now I'm not suggesting this should override your meticulous core speech planning and writing preparations. But it may allow you to make a few minor tweaks that could make a big difference.

CASE STUDY

Dr Patrick Dixon: How to read an audience

Influential business thinker Dr Patrick Dixon, often described in the media as Europe's leading futurist, is a proponent of taking the pulse of an audience before making a speech. 'Reading an audience actually, for me, begins the moment I land. I try to meet people, mingle, hang around the bar, turn up at the dinner the night before, which is really useful. I hate sitting down, because then you only get to speak to two people, so I try and wander round, stand by the buffet. I couldn't care about eating, I just want to chat. And often it's the anecdotes that you pick up at those points that can be magic for the following day. You could say, "I was just talking to Jeremy last night – where are you, Jeremy? – and Jeremy has given me permission to . . ." and suddenly you're in there as an authentic part of the whole conversation.'

Like me, Patrick considers it imperative to understand what's important to an audience and is keen to capture their stories. He's also very alert to the general mood and, whenever he can, tries to get a sense of that from watching his audience gather and converse in the lobby before going into the auditorium and taking their seats.

'You know straight away,' he observes. 'Is there a buzz? Is it subdued? What kind of relationships have they got there, what kind of personalities? It's absolutely fascinating. And audiences have very different personalities as well as cultures. I could walk into a group of risk managers and legal advisers for the banking industry, for instance. Or the following day, I could be talking to marketers or architects about smart cities. Oh my goodness, what different audiences! And nations themselves have different cultures, so you pick up all of those vibes. However well you prepare, there are things that the organizers don't always see, which I see the moment I walk in. So, it could be that the audience is a lot older than I was expecting, or I was told, or a lot younger. Or the audience is predominantly female, and I was expecting a mixed group, things like that.'

Adapting certain elements of your delivery, and possibly some of the language you use, in response to signals and cues you pick up through your interaction with audience members before you take to the stage could play to your advantage. Simple elements, such as using phrases or acronyms you have heard and which are familiar to the audience, reinforce the feeling that you are there to be part of their experience. Referencing audience members or earlier speakers and their content can also help create a bond between the speaker and the audience. These slight adjustments, especially early on in the speech, may make the difference between a speaker gaining the audience's trust and being quickly accepted as someone who is talking *with* them, rather than being perceived as talking *at* them. That sense of 'us and them' – or, more accurately for a solo speaker, 'me and them' – throws up a barrier to success. An audience who feels they are detached from the speaker and are being coldly instructed will not feel entertained. If it comes to that, the battle is lost.

Trust your gut instinct

While gauging your audience on the day is a sensible step, you must be careful not to seek out too many opinions at the briefing stage. Yes, everybody has slightly different opinions and expectations, but there comes a point of diminishing returns in information gathering. There's no cast-iron rule or formula to indicate exactly when that point has been reached, but good old gut instinct should help you here. Clearly, you don't want it to take up too much of your time.

There's also a danger that sounding out more than a handful of people could lead you to dilute the quality and punchiness of your speech by trying to accommodate the thoughts of too many others. Remember the need to stick to your core messages and personal brand in all of this. And make sure the briefing you pay the most attention to is the one by the organizer.

Ascertain the criteria for success

Finally, let me address one of the questions every speaker wants to get their head around in relation to a briefing. One that's fundamental to speech creation and delivery – the question of how to measure success. On numerous occasions over the years, I have seen instances where those people charged with providing the briefing are stumped for a good answer as to what success looks like. Sometimes how – or even whether – to measure has not been thought about at all. Which obviously is far from ideal.

In a professional setting, there is usually some sort of feedback form which will be used to judge audience reaction immediately after the speech. In a more casual setting, the yardstick may be the amount of applause and general audience reaction after the speaker's concluding words. However, when an organizer is looking for more than entertainment – perhaps they want the speech to kick-start a process of change, or evoke an emotion beyond enjoyment – the measurement of success becomes much more challenging.

Although ascertaining the criteria for success can be hard, it's important to try. If the organizer is not forthcoming on the subject, be sure to bring it up yourself in the briefing. You'll make the organizer stop and think, and the discussion that follows should help overcome potential misunderstandings and provide useful guidance. Before you get up onstage, you want to be sure that the speech you're going to deliver will be in line with the organizer's expectations.

But what if you're both the organizer *and* the speech maker? For example, you might be the leader of the team you're presenting to. Doesn't that make a nonsense of the briefing process? My answer to that is a categorical 'no'. Brief yourself as others would brief you. Be rigorous in your thinking about measures of success. It's too simplistic for someone in your position to argue that you just want your audience to have a good time, or that it's merely an exercise in letting the team know what's going on. You need to look beyond these superficial goals to identify what you want them to feel and learn as a result of your presentation. Even though you're the boss, for the purposes of your speech at least, don't forget that the members of the audience are the stars.

Speaking tips

- Find out as much as you can about the purpose of the event and the profile of your audience.
- Establish the criteria for measuring success.

6. Be at One with the Environment

There is more to great preparation than focusing on the speech. One critical element is often overlooked, and it's one that has to be addressed for any speaker to feel fully comfortable with themselves and the speech they are about to make. That critical element is the environment in which you'll be making your speech. And by this I mean more than just the venue.

Know the dress code

First of all, you need to be comfortable in your skin. There's a dress code for every event that helps in setting its style and tone – even in an internal company meeting, with its default to whatever everyday business attire would be for that particular organization or team. As the speaker you should, of course, take into account the dress code. Yet you should also be mindful of what makes you feel comfortable. Additionally, you should consider whether what you intend to wear will reflect the content and style of your speech. The question to ask yourself is, 'Does my appearance support my personal brand?'

Many events I have worked on, especially awards, are hosted by a comedian. As you'd expect, these are frequently black tie occasions. Yet a large number of comedians won't wear black tie, taking the stance that they need to wear clothes they feel comfortable in if they are to be humorous. I have never experienced a situation where the event organizer has objected to the host wearing different clothes to the dress code, nor have members of the audience ever commented on this. Both the audience and the organizer are more focused on whether the comedian is funny and great at hosting.

I have worked with plenty of speakers who are leaders in the fields of creativity and innovation. Often, these people insist on wearing clothes in keeping with how they think and act, which typically is more casual attire than that worn by the suited and booted attendees of the conference they are speaking at. They rationalize it with the argument that if they are thinking creatively (or, in these cases, talking about thinking creatively), they need to be in the right environment to have these thoughts. And who's to argue against that?

From a practical standpoint, however, there may be times when a degree of flexibility and compromise is needed. For example, if you're making a speech at a black tie wedding in which you'll be proposing a toast to the newlyweds. It would feel greatly out of keeping, and probably be frowned upon, if you were the only person in casual wear while everyone else at the wedding celebrations was resplendent in formal wear. But what's to stop you removing your bow tie if that makes you feel more comfortable? Trust me, people are much more interested in a good speech (delivered by a speaker who feels comfortable) than in staring at an item of neckwear.

This kind of behaviour is just as applicable to a business event. Take off your jacket and tie, if that will make you feel more comfortable and truer to yourself. It's about getting yourself into the right zone.

Know your physical environment

Now let's move on to the actual physical environment where you'll be delivering your speech. You are looking to create an environment for yourself in which you feel as relaxed as can be, and which enables you to connect with your audience in a manner that suits your delivery style and content. Taking the steps outlined below will make it much easier to focus on the delivery of your speech.

The best speakers make it seem effortless because they are at one with their environment. There are two elements to this – the venue as a whole, and the stage or speaking space itself. We'll start with the former.

The venue

The venue might be a meeting room, event space or conference centre. If you can find time to scope out the lie of the land before the day of your speech, this will be a tremendous help in visualizing your delivery. Even if you can't check it out first hand, make the effort to find out some details. Look online for any photos, ask the organizer, or call the venue.

The layout

The layout of the venue, and in particular the arrangement of the seating, can have a huge impact on a speaker's style and on whether you are able to successfully deliver a speech to the whole room. Some layouts are far more challenging than others. Experienced speakers alter their delivery style and use certain techniques in order to engage a room, depending on whether it is set up cabaret style (with audience members seated at small round tables) or theatre style (with rows of seating). Moreover, the size of the gap between you and your audience can massively affect the connection and energy levels – and consequently the success of your speech.

Given the opportunity, you should try to influence the layout of the room. Things you should ask for include:

- keeping the space between yourself and the audience to a minimum
- a clear line of sight for all attendees
- a clearly raised platform so everyone can see you (it doesn't need to be a stage but something that will elevate you so you can see the back of the room)
- the right lighting, for the audience as well as the speaker.

What works best for you is to some extent a matter of personal preference. Different speakers may like different layouts. Never be afraid to ask, or even visit the venue, so that you can be well prepared and in a position to influence the layout to suit you. If, for whatever reason, none of this is possible, at the very least give yourself time to acclimatize to the room ahead of the speech. Stand where you're going to be speaking and then have a good walk around. Familiarization beats the unexpected every time. Don't put yourself in the position where the first time you enter the room is when you're striding out to make your opening remarks to the audience.

The technical aspects

Next, we need to think about the technical aspects of the environment. Firstly, and critically, the audio-visual (AV) or sound and lighting. If the event at which you're delivering your speech has a professional AV team looking after the set, then these people are the speaker's best friends. They control the sound and any visuals you might be looking to use and as such play a significant role in ensuring the success of the speech. As a speaker, you should be making sure your new-found best friends are comfortable with your requirements and have been given all the right cues. You need to spend time with them, running through it all, so that you and they become a cohesive team for the speech.

The use of AV tends to signify the room is of a size that requires the speaker to use a microphone. You should be clear on your personal preference regarding this vital piece of equipment. Are you more at ease with a hand-held mic, lapel mic or headset? Tell the organizer which style of mic you want early on. There is no harm in making this request, as any decent organizer understands how important it is for a speaker to feel comfortable.

The staging

This brings us neatly on to the discussion about staging. Some people draw their energy from movement, while others prefer the security of speaking at a lectern where they have a place for their notes, and perhaps they feel reassured with their hands safely gripping the sides of the lectern. Generally, an organizer will have the stage set up in a particular way. Yet, as a speaker, it's down to you to make sure you're going to be placed in the best situation to suit your style of delivery. That means engaging in dialogue with the organizer to ensure your needs are accommodated. Just because an organizer initially envisages your staging one way doesn't mean you don't have the authority to change it. As with the mic discussion, if their hands aren't tied they should be happy to go with what works best for you. Just ask.

Nigel Risner: 'Animal theory'

Nigel Risner is a larger-than-life motivational and keynote speaker who specializes in human development and empowering individuals to play to their strengths in the workplace. He is known for his 'animal theory', expounded in the book '*It's a Zoo Around Here': The New Rules for Better Communication*, and when speaking often categorizes delegates according to four communication styles – lion, elephant, monkey and dolphin – to demonstrate how teams can benefit from the interplay of its different members.

Nigel always turns up early to check the room out and to make sure he and everyone else involved in staging the event is comfortable. 'As a professional speaker, I am hired to speak and if what you've got is an auditorium, that's what you've got, and you've got to get on with it,' he says. 'But if I had a choice and they ask me, "What would you like?" I will always ask for cabaret style. And I'll always ask for a gap so I can move around the tables. And I'll always ask for a slightly raised platform. But I don't want a big stage, as I want to be as near to the audience as I can.'

While some speakers want to keep audience participation to a minimum, Nigel is big on interaction. With that in mind, he's averse to a dark auditorium and always asks the AV team to light it, if possible, so that he is able to see the whites of people's eyes. He also has a speaker's toolkit that he brings to every engagement.

'I've always got some of my tools, and I also bring coloured pens for flipcharts and extra paper to put on walls,' says Nigel. 'As well as, for me, I always bring my animal hats. And I bring goodies to share with the audience. So I have a little case that always goes with me – and I don't ever check that bag in, because that's my security blanket.'

Ade Adepitan: Failsafe routine

TV presenter and Olympic wheelchair basketball player Ade Adepitan generally asks for the same things at every event, both because it's nice to have a routine and because if things don't go well it's then easier for him to look back and see if any part of his routine has changed. 'I usually talk to the hosts and let them know what I'm going to do and what I need to give them the best talk possible,' explains Ade. 'Unless there's a real emergency, I try to make sure what I get is what's shown on the tin.'

As a failsafe, to every event Ade brings his smartphone with reminders saved in the notes app, often including a specific point he wants to get across on the night, and a power bank for the phone. He also takes two USB sticks containing his presentation and, in addition, has a link to the presentation on his phone as a further backup.

In cases where you're set to deliver a less formal speech, such as to a team meeting, it still pays to consider the staging. You might not have the scope to rearrange the room to suit your preferred layout, especially if the room is dominated by a big boardroom table. But there are still little things you can do that will make a difference: for example, planning in advance exactly where you will stand.

Forearming yourself in this way diminishes uncertainty, which in turn reduces stress. It will help you feel in control.

Jon Culshaw: Lucky ritual

Some speakers also have particular lucky rituals that they follow. Britain's leading impressionist Jon Culshaw has a quirky routine he sticks to when speaking at awards nights and gala dinners.

'You know the place setting that has your name written on?' says Jon. 'For some reason, I always keep that. I always put that in my inside pocket, right at the start. I don't know why, it's just something I do. It's like a psychological connection to the event somehow.'

Speaking tips

- Familiarize yourself with the venue ahead of time.
- Ask for the room to be set up to suit your personal preferences.

7. On the Day

It's the day of the speech. You've done plenty of preparation, laid the groundwork for your speech to go well. You're ready to go. But what you do in the time immediately leading up to taking the stage can be critical and may make a big difference.

Accessing your comfort zone

The aim is to set yourself up in the way that works best for you. It's a case of getting as close to your comfort zone as you can. Yes, you'll still have some nerves – but because you're going about things in the right way, they should be at a level that helps rather than undermines your focus. When you come to speak, it won't seem as though you're battling through a tense finale. Actually, you'll feel an enjoyable sense of relief that will help the flow of your delivery.

Scope out the venue
As touched on in the previous chapter, the secret is to arrive early. That way, you'll get a clear sense of the environment. Take the time to check out the room in which you'll be speaking. Make sure the seating arrangements are in keeping with

your preferences, especially what was agreed with the organizer. And if an AV crew is involved, seek them out to remind them of the way you intend to go about things. They'll be happy to help – they want you to look and sound your best, after all.

Maggie Alphonsi: Feel the vibe

We discussed in the previous chapter how to sense the energy of the space and adapt to it. Former rugby union international Maggie Alphonsi, a World Cup winner and part of the England team that won a record-breaking seven consecutive Six Nations crowns, is arguably one of the most well-known names in women's team sports on the planet. Now a media professional and versatile public speaker, Maggie always aims to arrive early and attune herself to the prevailing mood.

'I always adapt my speech to the vibe on the day,' she says. 'I will have my core slides and videos, but I will deliver it a certain way, depending on the people in the room and the atmosphere. To help me understand the vibe I always aim to arrive early and listen to any previous speakers, and talk to any delegates or staff members in the room.'

Maggie doesn't have a pre-speech ritual as such, but she always introduces herself and makes sure her slides and videos are working. 'I also always send my slides to the client either a week or a few days before the talk, to make sure they have it and it's on their systems,' she adds. 'I also make sure I have a cup of coffee before I start my talk, to make sure I am alert and ready to go.'

Work the room

It's a good idea to strike up a conversation with other delegates, so you can drop in some teasers about your speech. Discussions of this sort not only allow you to gauge the mood of attendees – thereby enabling you to make a few tonal tweaks so that you're fully in tune with your audience – but also help to turn an unknown crowd into a series of friendly faces who have heightened expectations of a positive speech and already feel a connection with you. By working a room in this way, you're giving yourself a wonderful head start. Before even taking to the stage, you have begun to engage and excite your audience and get them on your side.

If you're speaking at an event which has speakers and sessions before yours, listen to some of the people who are on before you're due up. This will further enhance your knowledge of the audience.

CASE STUDY

Farrah Storr: Curate what you say

'It's always intriguing to take a seat backstage where you can see your audience,' says Farrah Storr, award-winning editor-in-chief of Elle UK, former editor-in-chief of Women's Health and Cosmopolitan and the author of The Discomfort Zone, a book that looks at how challenge and change can unlock creativity and human potential. 'It means you curate what you say. Are there lots of young women? Older men? Try and use anecdotes that will resonate with them, then.'

Absorb the context

It's a great idea to pay attention to some of the other speakers' key messages and the type of language being used through the day – whether that be by other speakers, or the prevailing industry language. It might be appropriate to mirror this kind of language, without overplaying it. This can bring a sense of continuity or familiarity to your speech, which will help draw the audience closer to you. It may even stir a vague feeling of kinship, a sense that you are 'one of us'. Certainly, if you use appropriate language, the audience will perceive that you understand them.

Moreover, fitting in by using some of these continuity tricks makes life a lot easier for an audience. They want to enjoy the speech, not spend time working out how it fits in with the rest of the day. If, as a speaker, you can help your audience connect the dots, that's another major step towards a successful outcome.

CASE STUDY

Cath Bishop: Keep it fresh

Olympic rower and respected diplomat Cath Bishop often speaks on subjects that revolve around handling setbacks and other tough situations. She's a firm believer in incorporating new messages heard during the day into her speeches.

'The more you can relate to things that happened in the event before you go on, or that are specific to the audience you are talking to, the more you can connect, and the audience will know you are not churning out another cut and pasted speech that you gave the day before,' Cath argues. 'It's particularly important to pick up on language used elsewhere during the event, so that you can reinforce and link with other messages, and again help the audience to understand the themes of the day, rather than making it hard work for them to link it all up.

'It also helps to avoid a gap between "internal" speakers and you as an "external" speaker, so that again, all the messages are mutually reinforcing and connected. It can also help freshen up your speech, so that you show how your stories and experiences are relevant to another organization.'

Cath treats listening to other speakers and leaders giving talks at an event as a form of continuing professional development (CPD). She aims to learn from the techniques they use to get their message across and often takes notes of stories that resonate with her. 'If I write down a few notes, then sometimes my mind automatically brings those into my talk when I get to points that naturally link up.'

Cath believes it's important to have a mindset of adaptability. She tells me it often feels to her that she adapts quite a bit, but in truth she says it's mainly only minor tweaks. Though 'sometimes those minor tweaks are critical to the speech feeling relevant to the audience, fitting for the venue and environment, and generally authentic.'

Preparing to go onstage

Many speakers have a set ritual they go through to get themselves in the right zone for their speech. This can help both to mentally position yourself in the right place and also to distract from the nerves that are no doubt setting in.

Now is not the time to be going through the speech again and again. The best time for practice is in the days leading up to the speech. You've done that and done it well. Frantically rereading your text in the precious last few moments won't yield any improvements. It won't help you memorize or deliver your speech any better. In fact, you're more likely to be engulfed by confusion and anxiety. So, don't fall into that trap. But you can focus on one or two key points or stories.

Staying in control

As the time for your speech draws close, find somewhere quiet to compose yourself and make any last-minute amendments. Now's the time to incorporate any points or language changes you've sniffed out doing your recce. It's absolutely critical to stress that you shouldn't be making wholesale changes at this stage. And you need to remain mindful of your tone and personal brand. Don't be tempted to embellish the speech with language you're not comfortable with.

If you have doubts as to whether something sits right in the speech, don't use it. When adding any new learnings or words at this late stage, satisfy yourself that they bring something worthwhile, complement the rest of your speech, and will help the audience. Gambling on the speaking equivalent of 'hit and hope' is not recommended.

CASE STUDY

Cath Bishop: Security blanket

At the outset of her speaking career, Cath Bishop used to write her speeches in considerable detail but her process has evolved over time. Now she plans a concise outline, usually to a maximum length of one side of A4 paper, and then distils that down into key points.

'I always have a record card with key structure, just a few bullet points, opening story and closing story, which I write within the last twenty-four hours, often on the way to an event, and which I look at in the final hour and again a few minutes before going on, and more or less memorize,' she reveals. 'I nearly always take the card with me on to the stage, either leave it at the lectern or fold it up small and put it in a pocket. I never look at it, but it's a security blanket in case I ever felt I had lost my way. Luckily, that has yet to happen.'

Devote the last few moments before getting up to speak to composure and control. Tell yourself the speech will take care of itself, because it will. Take this time to focus on giving yourself confidence. Remind yourself why you have been asked to speak. Reassure yourself of your credibility and credentials. Visualize what the audience will be feeling when your speech is finished, the impact it will make. This is absolutely the time for positive affirmation. Tell yourself you're going to nail it. Imagine a resounding round of applause.

Conquering last-minute nerves
Nerves, I presume, were one of your major concerns when you picked up this book. They loom large in the minds of many people preparing to speak in public. Indeed, it's probably fair to say they present the single biggest impediment for anyone thinking about delivering a speech. Now, moments before giving a speech, nerves will be at their most intense. They are not something that will disappear, however accomplished or experienced a speaker may be. The question is, how to manage

those nerves and turn them into something constructive? How to turn them into positive adrenaline which will feed your energy onstage and heighten your sense of what's achievable?

To answer those questions let me tell you a story from early in my career in the speaking industry. I was working with a high-profile speaker, a retired sports star, and having read a lot about them over the years in various publications, it was fairly clear that they didn't really need to do any professional speaking for the income. The first time they spoke, just before they went onstage, they were a bundle of nerves and energy. Then they went onstage and delivered a flawless performance. I watched in astonishment and decided the nerves must have been a one off. But just days later, I saw the whole routine play out again. This intrigued me no end. We chatted after the speech and I asked them why they put themselves through it when they were so obviously overcome with nerves beforehand.

The speaker turned to me and said how they feel just before they go onstage is the closest thing to what they felt when they were getting ready to perform at the height of their elite sporting career. They knew how to use their nerves to help them deliver the best possible performance they could. Nerves should not always be seen in a negative context. It is possible to reframe the way you relate to your nervousness and instead use it to help deliver something truly memorable onstage.

This, to me, is not ignoring nerves. It is definitely not minimizing nerves. Instead, it is making the most of your nerves by turning them into a catalyst for positive energy that will improve your speech delivery. Just like top athletes, who need the butterflies in their stomach before a race or match to perform at the highest level.

CASE STUDY

Farrah Storr: Reframe your emotions

Farrah Storr prepares by doing some stretching and deep breathing before stepping out in front of an audience. 'But I also tell myself that I feel challenged and excited, not scared. That's essential because most people, myself included, get the pounding head, the fluttering heart, the clammy hands, before they go onstage. How you interpret these feelings is crucial to how you will perform, however. Tell yourself you're scared and you can become overwhelmed quite easily. But tell yourself you feel excited – after all, excitement and fear manifest in similar ways in the body – and something remarkable happens. You breathe more easily, blood pumps round your body more freely, oxygen gets to the brain quicker, meaning you think sharper and smarter. It's been a total game changer for me.'

I've asked many brilliant speakers about nerves, over the years. There's a striking similarity to the responses. What they tell me is that, as the nerves build, the way to avoid succumbing to them is to focus on the first line of their speech. Once they have delivered that successfully, everything flows from there. And as if by magic, the nerves disappear. So, focus on nailing that opening line and you will deliver a successful speech.

CASE STUDY

Jon Culshaw: Switch off your fears

Comedian and impressionist Jon Culshaw says, 'Being nervous before making a speech, it's simply just fear of the unknown. You always find that the moment you start saying the first couple of words, it's not unknown territory any more. You're in that zone then, and the feeling vanishes.'

If a man as accustomed to performing as Jon still gets the jitters, you should expect them, too. When they arise, embrace them armed with the knowledge that they will help spur you on to a better performance and will evaporate as soon as you get going. Or, as Jon also puts it, 'that nervous feeling clicks off like a light.' That's a superb analogy that will help allay your worries. Calm yourself with a mental picture of your nerves being switched off as easily as a light.

Speaking tips

- Believe in yourself – you have the credibility and credentials.
- Tell yourself you feel excitement rather than fear.

8. Delivering the Speech

It's time to deliver your speech. After taking a final few moments to compose yourself, you're ready to knock 'em dead. The big build-up is at an end. This is the culmination of all the preparatory work you've carried out. Now it is down to the delivery. Buoyed by the time and effort spent on getting the speech right, you should feel ready for the richly deserved pay-off that comes from sharing your thoughts and opinions. And relieved that the wait is over.

Delivering the speech should be the culmination – and, indeed, the celebration – of all the hard work and time you've invested. Once you're into the swing of it, you'll feel in control. If you speak in a style that's true to you, and sits comfortably with your audience, the overwhelming likelihood is that you'll wow them with an excellent speech.

Let's now take a look at the process of delivering the speech in more detail.

Before you start

As you ascend the stage or head to the front of the room, shoot a quick glance at your audience. It doesn't matter whether you catch the eyes of a few people or glimpse a whole sea of faces, take that brief moment to reassure yourself that they are willing you to succeed. Because they are. Your audience want you to deliver a truly memorable speech just as much as you do. Stuck in their seats, they don't want to endure a dull speaker or struggle to make sense of someone who is unclear and incoherent. They'd be delighted for you to be great. So, remind yourself that they're on your side before you even open your mouth to speak.

CASE STUDY

Lord Coe: Avoid 'cookie cutter' speeches

'I think the audience needs to know pretty quickly that you've got a streak of humanity about you, you don't take yourself too seriously, and that you're not there to give a lecture,' says Sebastian Coe, prolific world record setter, one of the UK's greatest runners, Chairman of London 2012, President of the IAAF and keynote speaker. 'You're not there to read from a script. The one thing you need to establish really quickly is that this isn't a "cookie cutter" speech – it's not the same opening line with a slightly different name of the audience in it.'

Lord Coe adds that it's important not to be too aggressive or arrogant, and ideally you should make your audience laugh. 'Just put people at ease. Fundamentally, the first couple of minutes you don't want them thinking, "Oh my God, I've got an hour of this." You want them thinking, "Actually, the guy's quite relaxed about it, and I don't feel like I'm at INSEAD taking a lecture on management structures 101." '

The first two minutes

In Chapter 4, 'Telling Stories', we discussed how a good speaker can be flexible, often changing the flow of their story without undermining the purpose and impact of their speech, because of their confidence in and thorough knowledge of their underlying messages. That's tremendous. However, those opening two minutes are the opposite of that. They should be tightly scripted to deliver the points mentioned above.

One of the advantages of doing this is that it gives you a precious couple of minutes for your nerves, concerns and worries to be alleviated as you gain confidence onstage, in part because you'll see how receptive the audience is to your opening remarks. The words should be practised and practised so they can be delivered at the drop of a hat. You need to be confident that your remarks will engender respect and intrigue, and stimulate an appetite to hear more. You want to convey that you are well qualified to talk about your subject and have interesting things to say about it.

Sticking to tightly scripted messages during the opening two minutes puts you on reassuringly firm ground. It will help your confidence and flow as you get further into your speech.

The heart of the speech

It's crucial to establish your command of your material in the first two minutes, because you are not going to have a long-form copy of your speech up onstage with you. Ignore the temptation! In no way does that work. Contrary to what some people might think, having the full text to consult does not provide security.

Superficially, it might appear that the full script would be a useful crutch to turn to 'just in case' you forget your words. But that's an illusion. The reality is that the pieces of paper a speaker clutches act as a barrier between them and their audience. They weaken the connection and destroy the impression of a conversation, turning dynamic dialogue into uninspiring monologue.

CASE STUDY

Farrah Storr: Conversing with the audience

Award-winning editor Farrah Storr prides herself on being very meticulous in the run-up to a speech. She writes it out a couple of times, making sure the structure is as well executed as an expertly edited piece of writing, as this is how she personally best absorbs information.

'However, once I am on the stage with an audience in front of me I completely adapt,' she says. 'I don't use notes, never have. They can throw me off balance, and no one enjoys watching someone reading from a piece of paper. It kills the illusion that this is a natural conversation between you and your audience.

'Also, you have to work with the audience. A good speaker picks up on where they laugh, where they're silent and where the room dips in energy. When you feel that, you need to move your speech accordingly. If a swear word makes them giggle, you can slip another few in. If they go quiet, don't use one again!'

Cue cards

Please don't despair if you're worried about losing the thread. There's still scope to make use of an aide-memoire in the shape of prompt cards. The best way to go about this is to associate a word or phrase with each story or part of your speech. A series of prompt cards with 'trigger phrases' in the right order for the speech is all any speaker should need.

Taking this approach means the words you deliver on the day will feel natural and sit comfortably with your story. A quick glimpse at a trigger phrase, if necessary, and you're good to continue smoothly. Contrast that with the clumsiness of trying to find the line you're looking for on a busy page of text. Or worse still, getting sucked into just reading out one paragraph after another in a stilted, disconnected way. You'll seem about as warm and spontaneous as a police chief reading out a prepared statement to the press pack. Of course, you'll want to avoid going down that path! The art is to memorize the key points and then take advantage of the freedom to express yourself.

CASE STUDY

Daisy McAndrew: Breaking the ice

TV presenter, conference facilitator and awards host Daisy McAndrew insists it's essential for a speaker to find some way to break the ice. 'Sometimes it's a joke, sometimes it's as silly as a swear word, but it's something to show this is not a university lecturer giving a lecture to a load of rapt undergraduates. This is somebody sharing something with the audience, and it's finding a way of breaking that ice. Somebody will make a joke about themselves; some sort of self-mocking derogatory comment. They might make a joke about the organization. They will show they've done some homework. So, they will say something that makes it very clear that they know what this audience is all about.

'The audience think, okay – this guy – this girl, she's not just reading them out the speech that she does for everybody. She's tailor-made it. She gets us. She made a joke about it. Then she's made a joke about herself. Then she's done a namedrop to show that she does actually know what she's talking about, and now she's told us some fantastically indiscreet story about a politician.

'If you can do those sorts of things in the first few minutes, then they're on your side and they are willing you to do well.'

Visual aids

Now let's focus on another critical part of the speech: your slides or visuals. Never forget that they are there to complement the speech, not deliver it. Slides should be visually arresting and serve two purposes.

- For the speaker, they can act like prompt cards. The image displayed should trigger the story you've planned to deliver next in your speech – the correlation between image and story should be strong enough that it sparks almost instant recall of the association between the two and allows you to seamlessly move your speech along as envisaged.
- For the audience, the purpose is for them to glance at the image and mentally store it away before turning back to focus on the words being delivered. Assuming the image is striking, and the connection between story

and image is either obvious or highlighted, it will stick in their minds. And by so doing help certain key points of your speech lodge indelibly in the memory.

If a slide needs to contain words, my golden rule is that the maximum should be seven. Long enough to make a striking statement, but short enough that the audience is not distracted from the words being delivered by the speaker. Here's something so obvious, it's often overlooked: the audience is there to listen to a speech, not to read a slide show. Anything that takes the focus away from the speaker for more than a few seconds runs the risk of destroying that vital connection you must make with your audience.

A lot of speakers feel they need to display facts and figures on the screen. Both to reinforce the messages they are delivering but sometimes also to justify their credibility. This is not the way to go about it. Far better to make it clear to your audience that you can provide them with your slides and any accompanying fact sheets after the presentation. In this way, you can state facts without spending too long justifying them. But it also directs the audience to focus on the speech as opposed to the slides. It's preferable for you and for them that they don't need to spend time furiously scribbling down facts and figures shown on the screen. Instead, they can give you their full attention and thus enjoy the speech.

CASE STUDY

Dr Louise Mahler: One thing at a time

Dr Louise Mahler is a leadership speaker and body language specialist. She says, 'People can only focus on one thing at a time.

Which means that if you're using visuals and have a lot of information and graphs while you're talking, then you are deterring [the audience] from your own content!'

Slides, if you're using them, need to be of a high quality. Your slides represent your personal brand in the starkest way. However wonderful a speaker might be, if their slides portray a different image then the audience receives mixed messages. When that happens, a speaker runs the risk of compromising themselves because a speech is about the whole performance. So, if slides feature as part of your performance, you have to make absolutely sure the images you use deliver in the right way.

CASE STUDY

Nigel Risner: Doing without aids

Nigel Risner, once voted Speaker of the Year by the Academy of Chief Executives, cautions against over-reliance on slides. 'The best way to learn,' he says, 'is assuming that at some point in your presentation, the slides are not going to work, or the AV team are not going to do it, and you're just going to have to do without. I was at Sainsbury's head office and my slides didn't work – and it was one of the best presentations I've ever done. You don't know that you can do it until it doesn't work, because you think you rely on your slides. Your slides are an aid, they are not your presentation. If I could teach anybody anything, your slides are a bonus.'

Timing

Now, let's look at timing. Failure to tightly craft a speech means there is no control over how long it takes to deliver it. That could be a big mistake, because time is a critical element for any speaker. You need to understand and plan for the length of your speech.

When adopting a more freestyle approach to the delivery of your speech, you should keep a careful eye on time. Identify specific time points in the speech where you are delivering key messages for the audience and use these as markers: so, for example, Point A at five minutes in, Point B at ten, Point C at fifteen. One of the best things about making storytelling central to a speech is that it allows the speaker to make adjustments to ensure they finish on time. Think of it as a modularized approach in which you can alter the length of stories, or even drop one or two, without necessarily impacting the overall speech message.

Slow and steady

Finally, remember to take a breath onstage and slow down. A handful of great speakers are noted for their quickfire delivery, but for most of us speaking too fast due to adrenaline and nerves can make us sound garbled and tense. Cut some content from your speech rather than careering through it at a hundred miles an hour.

Don't worry about speaking too slowly, the audience will see this as you being clear and controlled. A speaker who speaks too quickly runs the risk of alienating the audience as they either cannot understand what is said or cannot keep up with it.

The end of the speech

Running over is bad. But running over and having to bring your speech to a hurried end before you've been able to deliver all your key points is a big mistake – and an opportunity missed. Many speakers deliver their key messages early in the speech to make sure they will be heard.

Running over is a complete no-no, for many reasons. For example, there could be a very tight schedule which is put in jeopardy by sessions or meetings overrunning. Or alternatively, the timing has been planned so that the audience don't start to get fidgety. It's more acceptable to finish slightly early, rather than late. Especially if you're leaving scope for a Q&A session (which we'll come to in Chapter 9, 'Turning the Speech into a Conversation').

What to do when you run out of time

Should you ever find yourself in a situation where you've mis-judged the timing, don't blurt out the remaining important points in a desperate rush. This is, in fact, the time to be honest. Explain that you won't be able to cover all the ground you laid out at the start of your speech. But make it clear that you'll be happy to talk about those missing points in the Q&A, and that you'll be around afterwards if anyone wants to discuss something with you then.

Your audience would prefer to hear an enjoyable speech than something hurried, where the content is lost in the delivery. Being honest will also strengthen the connection between the speaker and audience. This comes back to the speaker under-standing that the audience are the stars of the speech. They need to be involved in the whole of the speech, not just what the speaker decides.

Practice makes perfect

There are bumps in the road with public speaking, and the best way of ensuring they don't knock the wheels off a speech is to practise. Practice is everything. It's what helps you appear as natural as possible when entering an unnatural environment. The greatest speakers – those who appear to be able to speak 'off the cuff' – make no mistake, they are the ones who have spent hours practising.

The value of feedback

It's important to practise in front of people. Ideally, those you trust and whose advice you value and respect. Actively seek their feedback and encourage candour. Yes, it's great to get a confidence boost by hearing that you're good. But be sure that they mean what they say and aren't just trying to spare your feelings. Constructive criticism is a wonderful thing, as it allows you to pinpoint where improvement is necessary. The best way to gain confidence is through the practice and preparation in the lead up to the speech and in the quest for feedback that helps you up your game.

Honest feedback allows you to challenge yourself and greatly increase your chances of success. It will help you compare and contrast how you speak onstage versus how you speak in everyday life. You need to become aware of your speech patterns and delivery. You need to be in control of your body language and mannerisms. And you need to feel comfortable you are giving a true representation of who you are, not contriving a false personality, otherwise you'll be exposed when speaking and your audience will become confused.

CASE STUDY

Lord Coe: The art of a satisfying ending

And what advice for bringing things to a close? 'I think just really pulling the knitting together, not leaving it open-ended,' says Lord Coe. 'And fundamentally thanking people for taking the time to listen. They don't have to. Chances are, they're not being forced to be there. You know if they're at a conference, and there are other things going on, they don't have to be sitting in the room listening to you. Be grateful that they were there.'

Speaking tips

- Always remember, the audience is on your side.
- Prompt cards carrying trigger phrases can help you stay on track.

9. Turning the Speech into a Conversation

Up to this point, the traffic has all been going one way. That's in the nature of a speech. But here's the thing, the one consistent bit of feedback I have heard again and again over the years, from event organizers, audience members and speakers themselves, is this:

'The speech was fantastic, and really delivered what we were looking for from the speaker. But it was the Q&A at the end where things really took off. Wow! The questions, answers and discussion that took place elevated the speech to a place which was actually shared learning, and created real value.'

The skill to turn a speech into a two-way conversation is the greatest weapon in any speaker's armoury. It engages the audience. Even more importantly, on the assumption that you have the credibility and knowledge to keep on talking about the relevant subject matter, it means the audience can direct the speaker to the conversation *they* want to have. Not the conversation that you, the speaker, think they want to have. This is when you can deliver maximum value to the audience, who will be fully engaged in the speech. In this way, it becomes something memorable and impactful.

CASE STUDY

Kenneth Clarke: The joy of spontaneity

Former Chancellor of the Exchequer Kenneth Clarke, a lively, open and informative keynote speaker, relishes the Q&A dimension of public speaking. 'I prefer the questions and answers because it gives something to the speaker,' he says. 'Given that I do so many political speeches and so on, I know what my views are. I know that I want to argue in favour of them. I don't mind that, that's what I've been doing all my life. In a speech I know what I'm trying to get across. I know the case I'm trying to make, for whatever I think should be done, to the audience. And all that, I'm very familiar with it. What's interesting is to see what the reaction of the audience is. To listen to their opinions, as well as their questions. And it becomes more spontaneous. If it comes off, you engage with your audience.'

At the end of the speech: Q&As

In my opinion, all speakers should want to be involved in a Q&A after their speech – again, assuming they are comfortable with their subject. You'll probably find this the easiest part of your whole session, as you'll feel less 'on show' than during the preceding part of the speech. Think of the speech you've delivered as the start of a process. You want it to provoke thought, trigger curiosity, raise questions, whet the appetite to find out more. Don't treat it as a standalone piece. It's much more than that. It's a gateway to exciting exchanges.

Prompting the first question

You may feel apprehensive about announcing 'any questions?' for fear of being met with deathly silence from an audience who are unmoved and unmoving. Planting a question is a way around this. There's no doubt that, most of the time, it will kick-start the questioning by giving others the confidence to follow suit and speak up. However, I'm not an advocate of this sort of device, as audiences often see through it.

A slightly more nuanced way around the problem is to iden- tify a friendly face prior to your speech. Sound them out to see if they're willing and happy to ask you a question if no others are forthcoming. Greasing the wheels like this has the virtue of prompting genuine questions, despite the fact it requires a crafty nudge to elicit them, and it changes the dynamic in the room for the better.

Admitting lack of knowledge

Another major concern many speakers have about the inter- active session is whether they'll be asked a question which they're not sure about. Or whether they'll be challenged on some of the statements (or, even worse, some of the facts) in their speech. Once again, honesty will win the day. There's no harm in acknowledging a question from an audience member and offering to get back to them or to discuss it later. I'd go so far as to suggest this type of response endears a speaker to the audience and boosts their credibility.

An invaluable realization for any speaker is that while you might be a thought leader in your field – and, indeed, might even be the best person to make a speech about the subject matter – your audience does not harbour the expectation that you should know everything and have all the answers. No one presumes you'll be omniscient. Frequently, it's a case of getting the audience to think for themselves.

CASE STUDY

Lee Warren: Sit up and think

'The biggest insight I've had into Q&A, and I really do believe this, it's often the most interesting part of the session both for the speaker and the audience,' says professional magician and public speaker Lee Warren. 'In order to create that, as a speaker, you have to deliberately do two things. One is you have to be provocative – different people take that to mean different things. I don't mean being outrageous and I don't mean being rude, but you have to sort of get the audience to sit up and think, "Oh, I don't think I agree with that," or, "I haven't thought about that before."

'The second thing you have to do is you have to deliberately miss out information. Or you have to deliberately leave thoughts sometimes half formed, or not quite completed. And when I watch a really skilful speaker, I [see them] do that because it engenders really interesting questions.'

Generating dialogue

In order to stimulate questions, you might choose to purposefully omit a portion of content that would otherwise fit nicely into your speech. Ideally, this would be something obvious that can be used to spark interaction. One way to ensure that content gets an airing is to say something along the lines of, 'Sorry, I've almost run out of time and I know we need to cover this subject. Has anyone got any questions about . . . ?' This doubles as a way to lead people into the Q&A stage.

Your role as a speaker is to have opinions and thoughts based on your experiences and learnings. You should challenge assumptions and educate an audience. You should share ideas that instigate conversations. What's more, you should make it clear to your audience that they have a right to reply and that you truly desire and appreciate two-way interaction. While you want your audience to absorb the information you're sharing with them, you don't want a room of passive sponges. Rather, you're aiming for active listeners, feeding off the energy in the room as much as the points you are sharing, and readying themselves to participate in a dialogue.

CASE STUDY

Mark Jeffries: Authenticity and consistency

Mark Jeffries, a communications consultant for some of the world's largest businesses and previously a Merrill Lynch stockbroker, often speaks on techniques to build trust, success and connection. For him, the key criteria of successful public speaking include authenticity and consistency. 'People should feel that you are the same person onstage as you are off,' he says. 'And very often, Q&A is a more relaxed, more conversational affair and people can see the difference between you as a presenter and you as somebody handling Q&A. It should be the same. That's my view, anyway. Therefore, you are much more believable and credible as a person because you are not putting on a special act to be a presenter.'

Mark also has a tip for fielding the wrong sorts of questions. 'There's always someone who likes to make a name for themselves. They're probably there thinking, "I should be onstage," and they will often grandstand or make their question fifty-four minutes long. You just have to, in a very humorous way, handle that and keep things moving on.'

CASE STUDY

Cathy O'Dowd: Enjoy freewheeling

Intrepid mountaineer Cathy O'Dowd, the first woman to climb Mount Everest from both the north and south sides, enjoys the 'much more freewheeling' nature of the Q&A that comes in the wake of the 'specific and structured' journey she takes the audience on in her keynote speech, in which she wants them to experience certain stories she tells and certain points she makes. 'The Q&A afterwards is a chance to dig into the details of a story or an issue that caught the attention of the delegate,' she observes. 'Or to respond to their curiosity about something they've read in the media.'

Cathy adds it's fine to give a smile and a non-answer to the very rare question that is too intrusive. She also advises it's useful to have the master of ceremonies or the host on hand to shut down the session if one questioner is getting obsessed and the rest of the audience becomes restless.

During the speech: Real-time questions

The post-speech Q&A is the most obvious point of interaction. But as a true conversation is a continual interaction between two or more parties, it need not start and end there. A tightly controlled speech followed by a Q&A isn't the only model. Something more interactive should both excite and be the aim for any speaker. I say this definitively, as it's my belief that interaction strengthens the connection and bond between audience and speaker. This can only make the speaker feel even more at ease.

In the previous chapter, we looked at how engaging with your audience in those first two minutes is a good way to open. It immediately signals that this is an interactive conversation with everyone in the room. You can take this approach and run with it at various points during the rest of your speech. Asking an audience to voice their opinions, or give an indication of their feelings on a matter, turns up the energy levels in the room and makes people feel valued and included, rather than preached at.

However, encouraging questions throughout a speech is a tricky proposition. Audiences may be disinclined to take up the opportunity for fear of destroying the speaker's flow. From the speaker's standpoint, you must have a high degree of confidence in your ability not to be wrong-footed. Will you be able to return to the right position in your speech after being led off at a tangent?

Using technology to facilitate the conversation

As in so many other areas, technology is shaking things up. Apps are becoming more prevalent in the conference and live events space, enabling the audience to ask questions at any point during a speech. This is taking the world of speaking in a number of interesting directions. To begin with, audiences are becoming more comfortable with asking their questions in the moment, because doing this through the use of tech means they are not interrupting the speaker.

If the questions are accessible to the speaker in real time, this can be tremendously helpful. They give a great indication of the direction or topics the audience is most interested in. Embracing this, especially if you are telling stories in a modular fashion, allows you to adjust your speech and the time allotted to different areas in order to place greater emphasis on the stories and content that have struck a chord with the audience.

Technology has opened the door to more people asking questions. Whereas, in the past, some people would have been reluctant to engage because they were apprehensive of being in the spotlight, even for a brief period of time, today they can pose a question through the anonymity of an app. This has demonstrably led to more questions from people who wouldn't usually be asking them and has taken speechmaking further down the conversation path than ever.

CASE STUDY

Cathy O'Dowd: Embrace immersive technology

Cathy O'Dowd is among the speakers to have embraced technology to great effect by making it part and parcel of her presentations in a manner that immerses audiences in the narrative. She uses web-based polling software Mentimeter, which does mean there is an underlying risk that the tech will fail to work. That, she says, has become less common as the years have gone by. But she still makes sure she has a safety net. 'The presentation is designed in such a way that I can leave out the tech element without it affecting the rest of the speech. It also helps to have a few lines of easy filler dialogue on hand to plug the gap while waiting for the tech to work, or for the audience to work out what they are doing on their phones.'

Initially, event organizers were sometimes very nervous about polling. Cathy had a detailed PDF she could send them in advance, explaining the process step by step. That has changed in the last few years as such technology has become more reliable and commonly accepted.

'In the course of my story there are key decision-making moments; times when we, the climbing team, have to make a choice, despite not having enough information to be sure of the outcome,' says Cathy. 'By using polling software to ask the audience what they would do at this moment, I transform them from passive listeners into active participants, who now have a stake in which choice will turn out to be correct. Our team did not always make the right choices.

'When I first started using polling software, some people suggested it would be easier to just have a show of hands. But the two are not equivalent. People raise their hands, a public gesture, based on what their neighbours are doing, or what they think the boss would expect them to do. Polling is anonymous and private and gets a different result.

'Apart from the effect of making the audience active participants in the story, rather than just passive listeners, it helps to keep the presentation fresh for me. I know roughly what results I will get, but each audience is a little different, and it does reflect which industry they represent. Investment bankers and start-up people are heavily optimistic and risk tolerant;

insurance companies and legal teams are much more cautious and risk averse. And the voting results let me tease the audience gently in ways that they enjoy.'

Interaction spawns further interaction. To the enjoyment of everyone involved.

Speaking tips

- Think of your speech as a gateway to exciting exchanges.
- Make it clear that you want two-way interaction.

10. After-effects: Delivering a Lasting Impact

So that's it, the speech is done. You leave the stage or the front of the room, with applause ringing in your ears, and can breathe a well-earned sigh of relief. But while you may be thinking otherwise, the speech is not complete. Opportunities remain to shape and influence the audience. You have a chance to turn the speech into something memorable in the longer term. Some of the key things you said can make an indelible impression. Your speech can become greater than it was in the moments during which you made it.

We've discussed at length how a speech is composed of the stories you tell, and that those stories carry the messages you want to deliver. That said, different people will take different things from your speech, depending on their personalities, preferences and professional requirements – or to put it another way, what they find relatable and applicable. When you're onstage, your focus is on providing an enjoyable experience, speaking to the people in front of you in a language and style that's neither lecturing nor dull. You're mindful of connecting with them in the here and now. But you also need to plan for beyond this immediate experience.

Leave the audience with a clear message

The next step is to leave the audience with takeaways that are concise and can affect them personally. What these are is contingent on the nature of your speech, but it's paramount that they're easy to remember. They should tie in with the overall speech and leave the audience either wanting more or asking themselves questions.

Don't feel the need to deliver everything to your audience. Within a great speech, there is always an element of a teaser. Leaving the audience wanting more plays a part in leaving a lasting memory. Although a speech should always deliver substance, it should also hint at so much more. You are in the business of piquing interest, of creating demand for what you have to offer. Your audience should want to connect with you, either straight after you've spoken or through other channels in the following days, to find out more.

The value of a speech and its effects on an audience can continue long into the future, driven by individual members of the audience rather than the speaker. I know of many speakers who consistently receive feedback from audience members long after they have delivered their speech, sometimes years after the event. Often it's one distinct part of the speech that an erstwhile audience member recalls because it resonates powerfully with them. They have been left wanting more and, frequently, even after the passage of a considerable period of time, they still have questions they want to put to the speaker.

Continue the conversation

In the right circumstances, you should be clear that the speech was very much the start of the conversation. Invite a response from your audience and be sure to make yourself available in the subsequent coffee break and beyond to discuss any immediate thoughts. That includes being responsive via social media and other communications channels.

Having flagged up that you've started a conversation, you're almost duty bound to see it through. Don't frustrate and alienate audience members who subsequently make the effort to get in touch by blanking them – unless, of course, there is something weird or unsettling about their approach. Respond positively and promptly. They may simply want to drill deeper into your topic. Alternatively, they may have an interesting proposition for you, or prove to be useful contacts for the future. The fact they have taken the trouble to reach out indicates your speech has made an impact on them, and they may have had very good reasons for not buttonholing you on the day. Perhaps they had to hurry off to another engagement. It's possible they were shy about chatting with you in front of other people. Or maybe the issue or opportunity they want to raise with you is commercially sensitive and calls for complete discretion.

There is potentially a lot to be gained by showing flexibility and openness for the conversation to continue.

Share resources

There is one handy tip you can employ to help continue the conversation. Consider signposting for the audience any resources and reading material that will enhance their knowledge of the subject covered in your speech. The more you can demonstrate that the speech was the beginning, and not the end, the more opportunities you will create to achieve long-lasting impact. This may include sharing slides used during the speech, because these are a good way to jog memories of the stories you've told. However, it's generally best to be selective, if possible, rather than just sending out an entire presentation deck. And there are good alternatives to slides, which some speakers prefer.

CASE STUDY

Mandy Hickson: Postcards of change

'I provide postcards that can be popped on to a desk or fridge, just to remind people of the stories and to bring them back to the experience,' says motivational speaker Mandy Hickson. 'I don't think there should be too much material.'

Mandy fought hard to achieve her ambition to be a Royal Air Force pilot, becoming only the second woman to fly a Tornado GR4 combat aircraft on the front line, completing three tours of duty and forty-five missions over Iraq. She is very proud of the impact her speeches make, both in the corporate field, as well as on teenagers and their parents with respect to life choices.

'I have had many parents contact me to tell me what an impact I have had on their child,' says Mandy. 'Not necessarily in encouraging them to join the RAF, but more to find something that they are passionate about and to not be fearful of following their dreams. I share a story about a teenage girl, who was a very talented pilot, albeit at the very start of her flying career. It really seems to resonate, not just with other teenagers, but with adults alike, who have contacted me to say that as a consequence of listening to me they have made some vital changes in their lives.'

Draw a visual map of key ideas

In terms of takeaways, it has become more common in recent years for organizers to hire an artist to visually capture the key points of an event, which can then be digitally photographed and emailed to attendees. This is sometimes referred to as live illustration or graphic recording, with the idea being to visually map the key ideas of a conference and turn them into a snapshot summary.

When developing your own content it may occasionally be useful to visualize how some of your key ideas might be conveyed using such techniques. On the other hand, some experienced speakers take the view that it's better for delegates to draw or scribble down their own connections gleaned from your speech in pictorial or diagram form.

Explore ways to measure impact

From the client/organizer's point of view, how to measure or monitor the impact of a speech is a vexed issue. Whether the speech was liked or disliked is, needless to say, fairly easy to ascertain. But how effective it was, for example at driving change, is harder to pin down. Yet there are methods for evaluating outcomes. You may be in a position to track, analyse and further facilitate effectiveness after a speech. This is wonderful – and all the more so when it allows you to deepen your relationship with a client.

Nigel Barlow: A strange and unpredictable alchemy

'Naturally the client and their attendees – the audience – want to know some way in which they can assess the effect of the talk,' says business speaker Nigel Barlow. 'But get them to do it in an *active* way. I often encourage groups to come together a few weeks after an important event and tell stories about what they have acted on or found useful. Frequently, this peer inspiration helps others to both remember knowledge they have forgotten, and to see how their colleagues have made the concepts relevant and come to life in their application.'

Not all positive outcomes are quite so ordered, however. Often, speeches impact in unforeseen ways, provoking unexpected responses.

'This is often how it works: there's a strange and unpredictable alchemy that happens between a speaker's words and the reaction of the listener,' adds Nigel. 'What matters is not so much the message you think is vital, but how it's received and acted on. So, I was once surprised to hear that a Latin American company had built a whole advertising campaign around the words I used to describe having a more open, "possibility" mindset: think why not? What if?

'Recently, I was excited to learn that a delegate had been affected by my use of a psychometric describing his thinking style so vividly that he had changed jobs shortly after. He's much happier, and now is also a good client!'

The seeds you sow with a speech can flower into something unimagined. For the most part, though, the changes that arise should be in line with your goals. And you shouldn't turn your back on the opportunities to convey your key messages that exist after you've taken off your microphone.

Look beyond the finishing line

In the same way that you diligently prepared to give the speech – working on the content, the delivery, and feeling comfortable in the environment – you should be on top of maximizing the impact once you've left the stage. There's a lot you can do to enhance audience experience, cement your personal brand and embed your key messages. Let me draw a parallel with live music or theatrical performances. The band have played the last song of their encore, the cast of the play have taken their final bow. They leave the stage and the auditorium lights come up. It's all over, right? No, not necessarily. What if they then sign autographs and chat to fans at the stage door? They're giving their performance another dimension and making the night even more memorable.

Let me share a story that highlights the importance of the after-speech phase. I accompanied a speaker to an event and watched them deliver their speech. It went well, although I had previously seen this particular speaker achieve better reactions. However, afterwards they stayed behind and mixed and mingled with the audience. The feedback the next day from a number of delegates focused on what a lovely person the speaker was; it was only once they had spent time with them that they really appreciated the message being delivered. For me, this is the perfect demonstration of how a speaker is still able to impact the speech after they have delivered it.

To sum up, never equate uttering your concluding words onstage with crossing the finishing line. There's still some distance to go.

Create and deepen common bonds

I appreciate that this chapter has very much focused on sustaining the impact of a business speech. The other type of speech to consider is the more informal kind, where you will be looking for different sorts of outcomes. Generally, these speeches are made to celebrate or commemorate an occasion or a moment in time. The room might be full of people who know each other very well, or less so, and some of whom may not have seen one another for a long time.

The speech should bring people together in that room, to encourage the sharing of stories and reminiscing. Not only should it be inclusive for all, but it should be constructed and delivered in such a manner that when it's at an end it opens the way for you to 'work the room', using the anecdotes and stories shared in the speech to bring the different elements of the occasion together and create a shared experience. The communal thread of your stories should work as a focal point for discussion and foster a spirit of collectiveness. If you reference or expand on these stories as you're talking to people, you can maximize the effect of your speech to create or deepen common bonds between the different people attending the event.

In this way, you'll firmly lodge some of the key points of your speech in the memories of the people who matter.

Speaking tips

- While delivering on substance, a great speech should hint at more.
- Afterwards: mingle, underline takeaways, and follow up.

11. From Competent Speaker to Professional Speaker

My aim in this book has been to give guidance and tips that turn speaking into something all of us can look at in a different context: as a positive, shared experience, rather than one to be dreaded. By understanding how to stay in control of both the content and the environment, you can see the speech as something more relaxed and conversational than you may have originally perceived. As you gain more experience as a speaker, you will want to perfect your skills; to move from novice to professional speaker.

Clearly, this is a step up from occasionally being required to deliver an ad hoc speech when personal or professional circumstances dictate it. What I am referring to here is the group of people who, one way or another, are paid to speak – either by clients per speech they give, or by their employer because they are a spokesperson or an expert public voice for that company or institution. Often, people find themselves in either or both of these roles through chance. Few of us, I suspect, set the career goal of giving ourselves a platform from which to deliver speeches on a regular basis.

Why become a professional speaker?

The last twenty years or so have witnessed a rise in the pop star phenomenon of public speaking showcased by YouTube, TED and various other platforms. Its huge impact on the internet has spawned many imitators and competitors. It has raised the profile and amplified the voice of thought leaders and storytellers by broadening the reach of public speaking. Today, watching someone deliver a speech is something that's no longer confined to certain parts of society. Ideas, and the people who deliver those ideas, have ever more impact and reach ever larger audiences. They help us ask the right questions and form our own opinions in a world where clarity of thought is the truest of art forms.

Whether you choose to become a professional speaker or not, this chapter will give you a glimpse of what it takes to move from competent speaker to flawless professional.

The art of professional speaking

Working within the speaking industry, it's been my privilege to see many leading speakers in action. But everyone has to start somewhere, and many people have successfully navigated the route from competent public speaker to professional exponent of the art. With practice, poise and training.

Employ the 'rule of three'
One of the finest speakers of recent years is former US President Barack Obama, whose two terms in office were marked by numerous impactful and masterful speeches. Obama frequently made telling use of the 'rule of three' – the simple yet powerful principle that presenting ideas in groups of three helps lodge them in the memory of your listeners. Enough information to be interesting, but not too much to process and retain. Here are a couple of examples of Obama bringing the 'rule of three' to life.

'You can't let your failures define you – you have to let your failures teach you. You have to let them show you what to do differently next time.'

'Change will not come if we wait for some other person or some other time. We are the ones we've been waiting for. We are the change that we seek.'

As humans we respond to the patterns of the 'rule of three'. Obama made smart use of it many times to fire up audience engagement with his words and help his key messages hit home. Applying it with customary aplomb to writing and delivery is one of the factors that took the former President's speechmaking up to the next level.

Adapt your speech to your audience

To cut it as a top speaker you must also be adaptable and able to think on your feet. Ultimately, this boils down to having self-belief in your ability to adapt and carry it off. But this also includes developing the ability to read your audience.

CASE STUDY

Jonathan MacDonald: Attune yourself to the vibe

Jonathan MacDonald, a highly regarded keynote speaker who has created and executed commercial and digital strategies for companies globally, attunes himself to the vibe in the room while speaking and aims to pick up on the people who seem most engaged, speaking to that part of an audience more than others.

'If there is a set of detractors – detractors who are watching their phones all the time – I will maybe add in a two-minute interactive exercise where you speak to your neighbour about what the most exciting thing that you're working on is,' says Jonathan. 'So, I will read the vibe of the audience and actually modify in real time. And you do that by essentially watching their facial expressions, watching whether they're distracted, they're shuffling their feet, checking their phone, whether they're looking at the exits. People who are watching the clock either on the phone or their wristwatch tend to be thinking about what's happening next, rather than what's happening now, and there are opportunities for us to engage them all.'

Get plenty of 'true' practice

Unquestionably, the more public speaking you do, the better at it you get. A consistent refrain I hear from professional speakers is that the only 'true' practice they get is when they are up onstage doing it for real. That's when they can hone their craft and take themselves up a notch in terms of their quality as a speaker. By this, of course, I'm not contradicting what I've said many times in this book and suggesting that practice is futile. Not at all. It's essential. But to become an incredible pro there's no substitute for repeatedly getting up in front of an audience. To have been there and done that, time and again, knowing you are capable of reacting to whatever is thrown at you, boosts the confidence – of that there is no doubt.

Regard feedback to your speech – in addition to the questions posed by your audience when discussing your content – as a form of continuing professional development (CPD). Think of it as an improvement loop. Each circuit of that loop helps sharpen content and keep it up to date. The more feedback and interaction, the more you learn . . . and the better you get. The old saying has it that 'practice makes perfect', but that's not the case here. In the field of professional speaking, practice makes good; it's regularly delivering to an audience that makes perfect. The secret to mastering public speaking is to grab every opportunity you can to deliver your message.

CASE STUDY

Rory Sutherland: Returning to the stage

What happens if you're an accomplished and experienced speaker, but then don't do it for a while? One of the most interesting insights to emerge when I was interviewing prominent speakers for this book came from advertising guru Rory Sutherland. He revealed that if he takes a break from public speaking of, say, ten weeks or more, the first time he comes back to it after the hiatus it feels 'weirdly nerve wracking'.

Other speakers Rory has spoken with about this say they feel the same way, to the point that the nerves feel as bad as when they were just starting out in the field.

Stick to the fundamentals

It's important to stay true to the fundamentals outlined and exemplified throughout this book. You should always go onstage knowing the audience is on your side and keen to be entertained by the experience and carried along by your stories. They want your speech to be memorable for positive reasons. With that in mind, and staying true to who you are, you can give yourself a platform on which you feel comfortable. So comfortable, in fact, that the actual delivery of the speech feels as easy as speaking to your friends over a cup of coffee.

Learn from the experts

In the Appendix, 'Advice from Leading Speakers', there is a collection of top tips from great speakers who have turned public speaking into their livelihood. What they have to say will give you some insight into how they went from competent speakers to professionals. And how you can, too.

Speaking tips

- Hone speaking skills by learning from feedback and interaction.
- Grab every speaking opportunity you can.

---

12. Speaking in a Digital World

A whole new dimension in speaking has arisen out of the rapid growth of technology. Video conferencing and online meetings have been available for many years now, and uptake has snowballed steadily as technology and connectivity costs have fallen and bandwidth speed and reliability have improved exponentially. You've probably used one or more of Skype, Webex, Zoom or Google Hangouts, and there are plenty of alternative apps and platforms.

One major factor behind the increasing prevalence of video conferencing in business life is the expansion in working from home as part of the well-being efforts many employers are making to strike a better work-life balance for their employees. Another is globalization, with video connections bringing together individuals in different offices and often different time zones.

With the sudden and terrible outbreak of the 2020 Coronavirus pandemic, the steady growth of virtual meetings was transformed almost overnight into an explosion. Social distancing necessitated a fundamental shift in working patterns. Working from home was no longer unusual: for many of us it became the norm.

Virtual conferences and speechmaking are still in their infancy. Yet for many reasons they are sure to become more and more common for both business and personal occasions. There are great opportunities to be had in sharpening up your skills in this area.

Adapting to a changed dynamic

The rise of working from home means that more speeches than ever are now being delivered by a speaker sitting at a desk, staring at a screen. This, of course, changes the whole dynamic and energy of the room. It changes the interaction and relationship of the audience and the speaker. And it changes the speaker's ability to respond and adapt to audience reaction.

That said, whether a speech is 'live' or virtual doesn't alter the fundamentals of successful speaking outlined in previous chapters. But there are some differences in the way you need to act and prepare, in order to ensure video speaking achieves the same benefits.

I won't try to adapt every bit of advice contained in these pages – that would require a whole new book! However, let me offer some useful tips to help you become more comfortable with your new environment.

Curate your surroundings
At home, we sit at our dining-room table – or, if we're lucky, at our desk in a separate home office/study – and happily work. When it comes to speaking to other people via video, the chances are their eyes will wander while they look at the screen. Given the fixed camera set-up of a laptop, there's not really the option to pace around and generate energy through your movements (although I'm happy to stand corrected if you can figure out a way to do so). As such, the delegates watching and

listening will definitely take in your surroundings. So make sure that the environment befits the messages and content you are delivering. Be strategic about the backdrop and framing of the screen, whether that be pictures, books, and so on. Some video conferencing systems such as Zoom allow you to customize your virtual background. What you wear also assumes greater significance. You are being seen in close up and, as discussed, delegates will use the entire environment as a reference to either support or detract from the content you're sharing with them.

You should give some thought as to whether you want to be seen sitting behind a desk, or in an office chair away from a desk, which would allow a greater field of view for body language. Or you may prefer more informal furniture, such as a sofa. Each setting will make a different impression.

Familiarize yourself with the technology

To get the most out of speaking on a virtual platform, familiarize yourself with the actual technology you'll be using. Get to know the platform the meeting will be held on, ideally by doing some trial runs with colleagues or friends. This becomes all the more important if you are using slides, screenshares, or interacting through verbal or written questions. If this is your first interaction with this type of technology, practice and familiarization will improve your delivery and help keep anxiety at bay.

Create your own energy

Without a physical audience, the energy generated in a room by yourself is completely different to that of a physical conference or meeting room. Even so, the energy of a speaker is absolutely critical in the delivery of a speech and its success.

When delivering a speech to a camera as part of a virtual meeting, your energy comes from a much tighter frame than when onstage in front of rows of people. Onstage, your whole body and the movement generated by your actions – whether through hand motions or walking around – help generate energy. Further energy is generated by the people in the room, their physical presence and activity, and the 'buzz' going around.

In the virtual environment, that energy is taken away. For a start, the audience is many times more passive than even the most stony-faced live audience. Moreover, as you're probably sitting in a chair, you'll no longer be able to generate energy through whole-body movements.

The close-up nature of video speaking makes hand movements and facial expressions more prominent and pronounced. Bearing this in mind, you need to use your hands and facial expressions in a controlled way. Also, you should be really conscious of matching your body language with the words you express and the sentiments you deliver. You don't want to undo all the hard work of preparation with an ill-fitting hand gesture, awkward posture or a goofy gurn.

Focus on the build-up

There's no doubt it's a challenge to create your own energy on a screen in a room, usually alone. The build-up to video speaking is different. To begin with, you won't automatically feel that tight knot in the stomach typical of waiting to step out onstage in front of a bunch of people. But as we know, the surge of adrenaline that comes as you get ready to speak in a real-world setting plays a vital part in generating energy for your speech. When speaking on a virtual platform, where you're likely to be sitting down, you need to focus on your energy levels before you begin in order to give yourself a springboard. You're looking to force some adrenaline into the equation to kick-start your energy, allowing you to be lively and engaging when speaking, rather than dull and soporific. It may seem paradoxical, but the need to conjure up some adrenaline should leave a speaker feeling more drained and exhausted after delivering a speech to a virtual audience than when speaking to a room full of people.

Own your content

With video presentations, your content is absolutely critical. Ownership of the words and opinions you share is a necessity. Reading words that are not yours from a piece of paper (or even reciting them from memory), or making points that you don't truly believe in, simply won't work. There's no place to hide when the camera is focused on your face. You'll be under close scrutiny from your audience. They'll easily pick up on anything that doesn't ring true or seems at odds with your personal brand and how you normally behave.

Boost your confidence through practice

Another key difference will be the value of practice. No matter how much you practise, circumstances can always change when you have people in a room. Often for the better. Reacting to changes and adapting your speech in the room can play a major role in its success. However, for a virtual conference, you can practise in an environment which 100 per cent replicates the environment in which you'll be delivering the speech. Therefore, the role of practice becomes even more important to the success of the speech and in gaining confidence in delivery of it.

Prepare for success

The fundamentals of delivering a speech with confidence are the same, whatever the situation or audience. For the best results, you need to control the entire process, not only the time you spend delivering your words to your audience. That means the majority of the work relates to preparation and practice. There's no substitute for this, no matter how fluent a speaker you are, because the less preparation you do, the less likely you are to connect with your audience and have your key messages hit home. Quite simply, more preparation equals more impact.

Speaking tips

- Make sure the environment is in tune with your content.
- Familiarize yourself with the technology, doing trial runs if necessary.

Afterword

That's about it from me. It's been a pleasure writing this book, and I hope you've got a lot out of it.

Above all, I want you to have self-belief. You can do this, and do it well.

Perhaps I'll be in the audience to see you speak one day. If I am, you may well blow my socks off with your knowledge, passion and clarity. But whether I'm there or not, I wish you well in speaking with confidence.

Acknowledgements

Firstly, I would like to thank my partners in the world of speaking. My brother Tim, who has been alongside me throughout, at Speakers Corner and beyond, and has been my source of strength and fun through the ups and downs of our experiences in the speaking industry. To Michael, who joined Tim and me in our adventures with Speaking Office, thank you for being part of the adventure.

I would like to give massive thanks to the entire teams of Speakers Corner and Speaking Office, both present and past team members who have made the businesses what they have become and helped me to develop into the person I am. I would also like to thank all the speakers and members of the speaking industry that I have got to know and learn from during my years in the industry.

Thanks for all the help with the book to all the speakers who were happy to be interviewed and shared their expertise in all things speaking. I really appreciate all their time and effort. Also, special thanks to Rob Gray and my assistant, Poonam Douglas, who were integral to the book happening. I am absolutely grateful for all their efforts.

Finally, from a personal perspective, no words will ever be

enough for Nicky, Cally and Lola, who bring joy and happiness to every part of my being. The adventures and experiences we have together are the reason I wake up every day with a smile on my face.

Appendix: Advice from Leading Speakers

In putting this book together, it's been a pleasure to interview some of the finest speakers I've had the honour of working with, and to intersperse their thoughts through the chapters.

Here is a collection of their insights into the art of speaking with confidence. Enjoy what they have to say!

Jon Culshaw (hugely versatile impressionist with a catalogue of over 350 voices)

'You've got to know your audience. I always like to get there in plenty of time to get a sense of the atmosphere, get a sense of the mood, get the sense of who's there, what everyone talks about. I always join for the dinner at events like this – just to really absorb into it, so that when you go on the stage you're not a stranger. You will have picked up certain things and you feel part of the group, and it's always been the way I prefer to do it, to really just immerse and get in there. That's one thing that makes you feel more comfortable.'

Cath Bishop (Olympic rower, respected diplomat and versatile speaker)

'In my mind, I decide when I am going to "switch on" to speak. So, if I am early and can listen to someone before me, then I stay in relaxed, calm, listening mode, making notes, connecting what I am hearing to what I am going to say. I then automatically switch on – heart rate, adrenaline does it all for me! – with about fifteen minutes to go ahead of my speaking slot, or when they come and wire me up for a microphone.'

Ade Adepitan (TV presenter and Olympic wheelchair basketball player)

'No rituals, I just make sure I'm prepared. I'll probably do a quick run-through of the speech in my head about ten minutes before, go to the loo and then get onstage.'

Benjamin Zander (world-famous conductor and admired speaker on leadership)

'The reason that I never get nervous before I perform is because I'm so excited to share what I've discovered and to influence and inspire the people that I'm talking to. So, what happens when I get in front of an audience is that I get out of the way that it isn't about me, it's about them. And I'm looking for their response and their shining eyes and their excitement and their transformation.'

Colin Maclachlan (TV presenter of shows about the SAS and one of only a handful of people to have been involved in hostage negotiations, hostage rescue and been a hostage themselves)

'If you are talking from the standpoint of being an expert on something, make yourself human and vulnerable and, in some cases, ordinary. This may seem strange, but as a Special Forces commander who has led some high-profile missions, it is far better received when I tell stories of being afraid and up against it, rather than a cocky attitude of, "I was the elite soldier and nobody stood a chance against me." The "how" you deliver your core message is in many ways more important than the "what" your key message is.'

Farrah Storr (editor-in-chief of Elle UK, author and expert speaker on women's issues, leadership, and diversity and creativity in the workplace)

'I don't just trot out "my talk". I have a clear idea of what the audience in front of me is going through. What their challenges might be.'

Caspar Berry (unique keynote and motivational speaker who draws on his career as a professional poker player and successful businessman)

'I can remember a speech told to me twenty-seven years ago by Nik Powell, the film producer, who executive produced my first film for

Channel 4 and was a brilliant speaker and incredibly charismatic man. He did exactly this: he told five stories, and he actually said at the end of each story, "And I guess the thing that I learned from that was . . ." Literally just that structure of five things that I've learned from my thirty years in the film industry. And it was brilliant. One of the stories was dead simple. He went: "Virgin would have gone out of business [Powell co-founded Virgin Records with Richard Branson]. At one point we had no money at all and I remember vividly being outside the bank wearing my best suit, and Richard Branson turned up wearing jeans with holes in them, before that was fashionable, and an old jumper. And I said, 'What are you wearing?' and he said, 'No, what are you wearing?' He said, 'You look like a heroin addict at court, you look like you need the money. They'll never give it to you. I look like I don't need the money and they'll give it to me.' And I guess what I learned from that was . . ." So that's a little story, right? Man wants money. Virgin's about to go out of business, so we've got some consequence of the downside, and he learns a lesson from a guy who takes a counter-intuitive reversal position. He literally just had about five stories like that that probably lasted about six or seven minutes each. If you had a blank slate and you were going to do a speech, I would just do that.'

Gemma Milne (award-winning science and technology writer and podcaster)

'The audience wants to enjoy your talk, and they want to learn something from you, and they want you not to be nervous. They're on your side, they're not a bunch of lions pouncing on you. They are a lot of kittens looking up to you like, "What have you got to say?" They're your pals; remember that, and treat them as such. And find pals in the audience, find the people who are nodding loads and just focus on them, jump between them. The people who nod tend to be speakers themselves. I nod at people's talks because I know that it gives people confidence. It's not a deliberate thing, it's kind of just automatic. Also you give people attention if you do that. If you're in the audience and you're nodding, the speaker will come speak to you after, normally. It's quite a good way of getting their attention. Anyway, find your nodders and they will be rooting for you.'

Javier Bajer (cognitive psychologist who has been instrumental in some of the world's largest mergers, bringing people together as a priority above technology)

'Of course, as a speaker, I want them to remember me, because they'll call me back and they'll adulate me for a while, so there is a human side which will say me, me, me: get to my website and buy my book. In reality, when I'm not needy – which is hopefully most of the time – what's more important is that they change something important in their lives.'

Jonathan MacDonald (expert in disruptive innovation, changing business models and future trends)

'After the briefing call, I continue to track any mention of the brand, any new launch or any movements of the brand – executives leaving, joining, whatever. I continue to track up until the day of the event, and for that tracking I use Google Alerts. That's free of charge to do, and you can temporarily set one up and delete one, so it's not a hardship. And I always ask, and clients love this, if I can arrive early to get the feeling of the event.'

Kenneth Clarke (former Chancellor of the Exchequer and Home Secretary)

'I find that I'm better when I don't carefully script it. And I rarely have notes. If the subject is a serious subject, I may have little headings because, if I'm not careful, if I do it spontaneously, then I might leave something out completely. So, little subjects; what I'm going on to next.'

Lee Warren (professional magician and mind-reader who shares the secrets to being an outstanding communicator in the world of business)

'One of my themes is persuasive psychology, to help people be more compelling, more engaging. So, for me, it's lovely if an audience member puts their hand up and they say, "While you've been talking, I've been thinking; I've got this big pitch to do tomorrow and what do you think about . . . ?" and they'll tell me about their situation briefly. That's a genuinely collaborative thing where that audience member is going to leave that session better than when they went in. And I'm going to leave feeling better than I did, had I not had that question.'

Mark Jeffries (communications consultant for some of the world's largest businesses)

'You can absolutely make a great impact with a keynote or a speech and then leave the stage, head off and have made a wonderful and lasting impact with that group. But if you do engage in Q&A, and you do make it more interactive, there is definitely a stronger bond between you and them. They will remember you more fondly because they were able to get involved and, most importantly, be heard.'

Miles Hilton-Barber (adventurer whose many epic feats include becoming the first blind pilot to undertake a 55-day, 21,000 kilometre microlight flight from London to Sydney)

'Look, if I leave an audience thinking how amazing I was, and how rubbish they were, I've totally failed. But if I can leave them thinking, "Wow, what an ordinary guy, ups and downs just like me, and actually I think I could do more . . ." I don't want to be on the pedestal, I want them to be on the pedestal, looking around, thinking I could do a lot more. There's a lovely Jewish proverb: "Silver is refined in a furnace and gold by fire. And a man is refined by his praise." Basically, if you want to know what's inside a guy, just surround him with praise and adulation and you'll see whether that's him thinking, "Well, that's of course what I deserve." And pride comes before a fall. You're on a slippery slope as soon as you start believing that you're some big guy and everyone owes you a living – or an ear.'

Nick Jankel (has spent twenty-five years cracking the code on breakthrough change and how to use science, wisdom and entrepreneurial tools to hack through hearts, minds and culture)

'You actually have to think about your story backwards. Which is, what's the behaviour change? What's the mindset change? And now, given I've got three minutes, or five minutes or ten minutes or half an hour, what are the essential things people need to hear to get them from A to B? You have to realize that people aren't cognitive machines that just need to hear a message and then they change. They have emotion, and therefore part of your story has to shift them emotionally so they can even hear the message. Because if they're resistant or not interested or tired or stressed out, or thinking you're just not a great person, then they're not even listening to the message. They're closed off. So, your story then has to build an emotional change, not just a cognitive message, to get people to walk away with anything.'

Nigel Risner (motivational and keynote speaker and specialist in human development, known for his 'animal theory')

'I'm spending my whole time looking at audience reaction to see who's following what I'm saying and is the energy right. And if I have to change. I've done it a few times recently – I've had to ramp up the energy because it's the session after lunch and I can see that dozy look and that glazed-eye look.'

Dr Patrick Dixon (often described in the media as Europe's leading futurist and has been ranked as one of the twenty most influential business thinkers alive today)

'Stick to the things you're passionate about. If you're using PowerPoint, strike out every slide you wouldn't die for. Because if it doesn't matter to you, why for goodness' sake inflict that on an audience? If it doesn't matter to you, why on earth should it matter to anybody else? Just take it out, junk it. Stick to the things you are passionate about. Let your passion shine, and we will listen to you and you will be heard with dignity to the very last word, and you will hear a pin drop.'

Rory Sutherland (has had an illustrious career in advertising, marketing and branding)

'Occasionally, I'll go off on digressions, I'll occasionally go on complete non sequiturs where I'm not even sure myself where it's going. The reason I do that is because the feeling that anything could happen now holds the attention. If you have a presentation from someone, particularly if it's from a team, where it's clear that the team have researched everything themselves, or between themselves, several times in advance, it feels like going through the motions. It's like a religious ceremony where you're just rehearsing a creed, rather than saying something fresh. I think if you're comfortable in your material, you can riff. And I think riffing a bit suggests that you know what you're on about.'

Lord Coe (prolific world record setter, one of the UK's greatest runners, Chairman of London 2012, President of the IAAF and keynote speaker)

'Spend time trying to understand the group or the business you're talking to. There's nothing worse than being in an audience where you know that the same speech was probably given five hours ago to another organization up the road. Make it your business to really understand who they are, what are their ambitions, what was the environment around the time that business was created. If it's thirty years ago, familiarize [yourself] and understand what was going on in the world then. If it was 1968/69, for instance, you know it's moon landings, it's riots in Paris, you know that it was a Labour government heading towards Ted Heath, you know the Vietnam War, you know Selma, you know what was going on on American university campuses. You want to be able to contextualize. Often, we're asked to go and speak to an organization that's celebrating its fortieth or its fiftieth or its twenty-fifth anniversary. Find out what was going on that year. Just show that you've made an effort to personalize it, rather than just going: "I can do this in my sleep and all I've really got to master is making it sound fresh." It won't cut it.'

Will Butler-Adams (boss of Brompton Bicycle and Brompton Bike Hire)

'My feeling, in the first minute, is actually to be quiet and slow down. You have a propensity to start a talk at a hundred miles an hour. Really firm and loud. And actually, I've found that when I get onstage, I start slightly modestly and I build it up. Because they're expecting me to jump onstage and go, "RAH, RAH, RAH!" So, when I come up onstage and say, "Hi, my name is . . ." and I start slowly, it gets them to listen. Because you're not quite so loud, and you're not quite so in their face, they listen. And then you build them up, and then you have a crescendo, and then you drop them down, and then you bring them up again. But turn up and start barking at people, I actually think that's quite the opposite [of what you should do].'

Tanni Grey-Thompson (Britain's most successful Paralympic athlete in wheelchair racing, awarded the prestigious honour of a DBE for services to sport in 2005)

'One thing I spoke at a while ago, they said, "Everyone will be really drunk and it's a huge celebration and they're a very warm audience." But I was presenting some awards, and they said, "You basically have to tell them to be quiet all the time," and I was like, "Really? That's a bit bossy and a bit rude." I was just like, "Shhhh!" It wasn't off-putting, because it was a really warm environment – a warm atmosphere – and everyone was having a really nice time. So, listen to what people say, because I think if I hadn't been prepared by the client [saying], "This is a massive evening for everybody who comes. They actually do celebrate everyone, even if they haven't won an award," it would have been a little bit daunting going into that.

'So, for me, [it's worth] just asking, "What would you like to see happen that you haven't in the past? What maybe hasn't worked?" They don't have to give specifics. Things like: what's the average age of the audience? To make sure that, if you're using any cultural references, it connects to the audience. It's asking quite simple questions. If you're speaking in front of an international audience, there's no point using references that are very specifically British – it's not rocket science, it's really not.'

Jez Rose (a magician, comedian and speaker who has entertained audiences in more than twenty-three countries; also sometimes known as 'The Unusualist')

'I thought very carefully when I created a brand around my speaking work, taking a lot of time to consider what it should be, what it shouldn't be, and what my clients needed it to be. I remember it being quite a challenging task. The first iteration of a serious brand I had was "The Behaviour Expert", in response to the colloquial nickname my clients gave me, due to my consultancy and training work with them as a Behaviour Insight Adviser. Recently, I rebranded, using my name, Jez Rose, and losing The Behaviour Expert. They say very different things and represent different periods of my life. The current brand, using only my name, sits much clearer with my broadcast work in television and radio, as that is my identity, but also allows me to position topics and content that are more genuine and sincere to my own thinking and beliefs right now.'

Maggie Alphonsi (the face of international women's rugby and arguably one of the best-known names in women's team sports)

'Over time, I have developed my talks to be more practical, and I engage more with the audience. Previously, I would just speak at the audience. But now I seek their thoughts and use them to create discussions.'

Mandy Hickson (former Royal Air Force pilot and the second woman to fly the Tornado GR4 operationally, completing forty-five missions over Iraq)

'No speakers can hold all the answers, but they can share their stories. One of the most frustrating aspects that many delegates describe is when a speaker is talking to an audience from a very different industry to their own, and they try to shoehorn their messages in, or to explain why this is relevant to the audience. They hate it! Generally, we are speaking to highly educated groups who can make this leap very easily themselves and they don't need to feel patronized in the process. I do believe it is important to hold your own opinions, though, and be happy to share these honestly and with full transparency.'

Mark Schulman (a drummer and cellist who has performed with a galaxy of music stars, and helps audiences unlock their rock star attitude while providing practical, innovative business strategies)

'I have seen some of the greatest speakers use no media at all. Conversely, when I've seen speakers use a lot of media, I have found myself getting distracted and not always walking away with a clear understanding of the content. Less can be more. If a speaker feels strongly about critical information that they believe will truly enhance their presentation with a visual representation, then pause and let the audience read and absorb the information. Then speak once they have. That's a way to ensure that they get to focus on one thing at a time!'

Daisy McAndrew (broadcaster, popular conference facilitator and awards host)

'Make it really obvious that you've finished. It's really easy, even if the speech hasn't gone well – which it will do, because you will have read this book! You can still end on a high just by lifting your head up, maybe putting your arms up and saying, "Ladies and gentlemen, thank you so much for . . ." Practise that last bit. You've got to practise it and do it big, because it's not that you're asking for applause, you're doing the audience a favour by not embarrassing them. You've got to tell yourself that's why you're doing this grandiose gesture, because that's actually the last thing they will remember. And when they fill in the forms about whether you were any good or not, and whether you are invited back . . . "Well, it was good but then it petered out. I didn't know whether to clap, and then I was embarrassed and I looked at the floor, and I couldn't make eye contact with them because it felt really flat." You can ruin a whole speech by a bad final five seconds.'

Cathy O'Dowd (the first woman to climb Mount Everest from both the north and south sides)

'Q&A can be fun, and some audiences clearly love it. Sometimes it takes a few minutes for the audience to warm up. So I discourage, "Just one or two questions." Either don't do it, or have five or ten minutes set aside for it. I often find that what seems like one or two hesitant questions in the first minute turns into a flood, five minutes in. I also have a line I tend to use to acknowledge and tease that awkward silence as everyone waits for someone else to be the first to put their hand up. It seems to help to ease the tension.'

Debra Searle (adventurer, businesswoman and gender equality advocate who has rowed solo across the Atlantic)

'Afterwards, there's a number of ways that you can know it's worked: whether you get people coming up to you to speak to you is always a really big indicator. And when people speak to you afterwards, when they pick up on bits they really found helpful in your speech, do they relay it word for word? The reason I say that is because when we give key messages, it's crucial that there's a lot of repetition in the key message. You can't just say it once, because people won't remember it. For example, one of the things I talk about a lot is, "Choose your attitude." And if I haven't said it enough throughout the speech, people come up and they kind of get it right, but they don't quite get it right. They might say, "Choose what you think about." They'll say something like that, and you'll think, "Okay, so I didn't actually repeat it enough." '

Nigel Barlow (an advocate of thinking differently, collaboration and innovation through disruption)

'The best take-home materials are visual and brief, ideally created by the delegates themselves. The old technique of Mind Mapping, originally invented by Tony Buzan, is to be encouraged. Because the very act of sifting information and capturing it with keywords, colour and images during a talk ensures the most powerful gift a listener has; their attention fully engages with the material as it is put over.'

Index

PENGUIN PARTNERSHIPS

Penguin Partnerships is the Creative Sales and Promotions team at Penguin Random House. We have a long history of working with clients on a wide variety of briefs, specializing in brand promotions, bespoke publishing and retail exclusives, plus corporate, entertainment and media partnerships.

We can respond quickly to briefs and specialize in repurposing books and content for sales promotions, for use as incentives and retail exclusives as well as creating content for new books in collaboration with our partners as part of branded book relationships.

Equally if you'd simply like to buy a bulk quantity of one of our existing books at a special discount, we can help with that too. Our books can make excellent corporate or employee gifts.

Special editions, including personalized covers, excerpts of existing books or books with corporate logos can be created in large quantities for special needs.

We can work within your budget to deliver whatever you want, however you want it.

For more information, please contact
salesenquiries@penguinrandomhouse.co.uk